BLACKBURN TO SKIPTON

including Stubbins Junction to Accrington, the Padiham Loop and Barnoldswick Branch

Mark Bartlett

MP Middleton Press

To Gayle – for all those long hours by the railway waiting for yet another train.

Front cover: Colne, towards the end of steam. A Black 5 arrives from Rose Grove to take 3P20, the evening parcels to Preston. The cleared area to the right was the site of the Midland engine shed. Once busy sidings on the left are gradually seeing less and less use, although for the time being there are two parcels trains a day from here, sometimes more. An 8F on an engineer's train is heading tender first towards Burnley, the wagons filled with sleepers, perhaps from the closed Barnoldswick Branch. The Black 5 will go into the sidings, bring out the parcels vans and then go on the front for departure. Colne North signal box is in the foreground. Today, where the signal box and loco were, is a busy road leading from the motorway to Colne. (Donald Speak)

Back cover:

***Upper:** Two Cravens DMUs meet at Huncoat station in the early 1960s. The diesel hydraulic set on the right (later class 113 - identified by the large headcode box) is heading for Blackpool Central while the standard (later class 105) set is heading towards Colne. The author's earliest railway memories are of Huncoat. WD 2-8-0s clanking through on coal trains and trips on the Cravens DMUs, with their curved back seats, to Todd Lane for family visits. (ColourRail.co.uk)*

***Middle:** The enamel signs were located in the Burnley Barracks ticket office, directing passengers down the stairs or across the footbridge.*

***Lower:** Railway Clearing House map, dated 1947. The route of this album is shown with a dotted line.*

ACKNOWLEDGEMENTS

I am very grateful for the assistance of Roy Davies, Malcolm Chattwood, Chris Leach – L&YR Society and Ewan Crawford – Railscot, Cass and Deb at Middleton Press, and also to Geoff Gartside, Chris Howard, Norman Langridge, Brian Read (gradient profiles) and David and Dr Susan Salter.

I am also grateful to all the photographers and collection owners who have made their photographs available for use in this album.

Published May 2024

ISBN 978 1 910356 85 2

Cover design and Photographic enhancement Deborah Esher
Production and design Cassandra Morgan

Published by
Middleton Press Ltd
Camelsdale Road
Haslemere
Surrey, GU27 3RJ
Tel: 01730 813169
Email: info@middletonpress.co.uk
www.middletonpress.co.uk

Printed and bound by CPI Group (UK) Ltd, Croydon, CR0 4YY

Abbreviations:

Blackburn, Burnley, Accrington & Colne Extension Railway (BBA&CER)
Blackburn, Clitheroe and North West Junction Railway (BC&NWJR)
Blackburn and Preston Railway (B&PR)
Bolton, Blackburn, Clitheroe and West Riding Railway (BBC&WRR)
British Railways/British Rail (BR)
Coal Concentration Depot (CCD)
East Lancashire Railway (ELR)
East Lancashire Railway Preservation Society (ELRPS)
Fleetwood, Preston and West Riding Junction Railway (FP&WRJR)
Lancashire and Yorkshire Railway (L&YR)
Leeds and Bradford Extension Railway (L&BER)
London Midland and Scottish Railway (LMS)
London Midland Region (LMR)
Manchester, Bury and Rossendale Railway (MB&RR)
Midland Railway (MR)
North American Coal Corporation (NACCO)
Rail Accident Investigation Branch (RAIB)
Working Timetable (WTT)

SECTIONS

CONTENTS

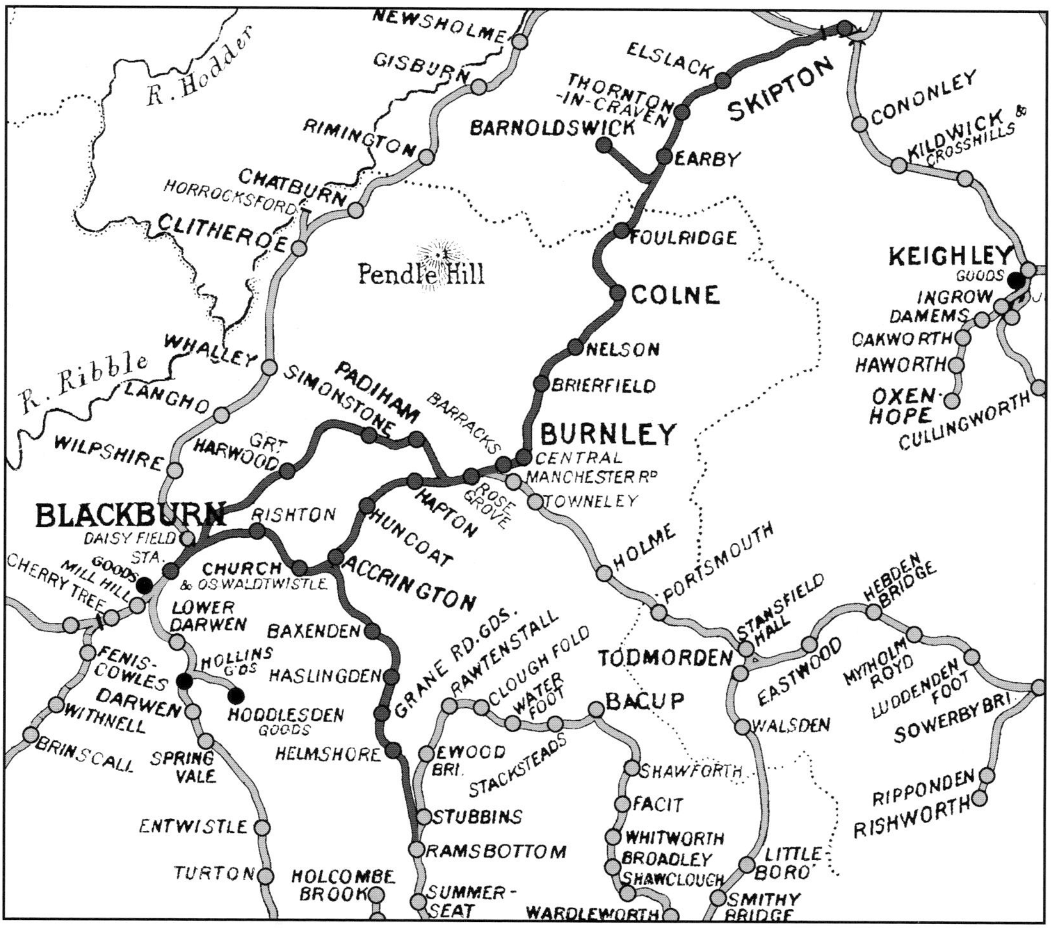

I. The Railway Clearing House map (edited) of 1947 has the route of this album in dark grey.

GEOGRAPHICAL SETTING

Travelling eastwards from Blackburn trains wind through East Lancashire towns and countryside. The surrounding hills are always in sight but the undulating line has no taxing gradients. Today the M65 and the Leeds and Liverpool Canal closely follow much of the route between Blackburn and Colne. The Padiham Loop generally ran eastwards to the north of the surviving line, through deep cuttings and over high embankments and viaducts. It dropped down from the junction on a 1:90 gradient to Great Harwood and then ran along the valley of the River Calder but had to climb a 1:40 incline for one mile from Padiham to join the main line again at Rose Grove. Steep gradients were the norm for most of the Stubbins Junction to Accrington route, which ran generally south to north. By contrast the closed Midland section beyond Colne rose gently to Foulridge before an equally gentle north easterly descent towards Skipton. All these lines serviced the Lancashire cotton industry, while the main route ran through the Burnley Coalfield and served a number of its collieries, in addition to the brick works which were established around high quality clay deposits between Accrington and Huncoat. In later years, three power stations were built alongside these lines, and rail served until closure.

All maps in the album are derived from 25ins to 1 mile editions dated 1909-12, with north at the top, unless otherwise indicated.

HISTORICAL BACKGROUND

A summary of these lines might be that the Lancashire and Yorkshire Railway had several routes that converged end on with the Midland route from Skipton at Colne. Their history of course is more complicated as these large pre-grouping railway companies took over various lines whose promoting companies had been absorbed by ever larger railways.

Chronology of openings

Lines between Blackburn and Colne and between Stubbins and Accrington were promoted in the early 1840s by the Manchester, Bury and Rossendale Railway (MB&RR), the Blackburn and Preston Railway (B&PR) and the Blackburn, Burnley, Accrington & Colne Extension Railway (BBA&CER) but before any of these railways actually opened these three companies had merged to form the East Lancashire Railway (ELR) in 1845. The ELR went on to expand further acquiring a route to Liverpool through Ormskirk but eventually amalgamated with the Lancashire and Yorkshire Railway (L&YR) in 1859.

The Clifton to Bury and Rawtenstall line, originally promoted by the MB&RR, was inaugurated on Friday 25th September 1846 and opened to traffic the following Monday.

The BBA&CER proposed to extend the line from Stubbins Junction to Accrington from where it would go west to meet the B&PR at Blackburn and east through Burnley to Colne. Their Bill for this proposed line received Royal Assent on 30th June 1845.

After working together the companies formally joined on 3rd August 1846 to form the East Lancashire Railway. Work progressed towards a planned opening date, through to Colne, on 1st January 1848. However, there were construction difficulties, not least with the long viaduct between Burnley Barracks and Burnley Central stations, where, in 1846, an arch collapsed during building work. Eventually the line from Stubbins Junction, to a triangular junction at Accrington,

—	**Blackburn** ....dep.		5 27	6 2	6 22	6 38	....	....	7 52	7 55	8 5	8 23	....	8 41	....	....	8 54	9 15	9 34	9 37	10 4	....	1016	....	....	....	11 9	1117	....	1210	1215	1 8
38	Rishton	....	5 35	6 10	Via Padiham.	....	....	....	8 0	Via Padiham.	....	....	....	8 48	....	....	9 2	9 22	Via Padiham.	9 45	Via Padiham.	....	1024	....	....	....	1116	Via Padiham.	....	....	1223	1 16
39½	Church & Oswaldtwistle..	....	5 39	6 14		....	....	....	8 4		8 14	....	....	8 52	....	....	9 6	9 26		9 49		....	1028	....	....	....	1120		....	....	1227	1 20
40½	**Accrington 785** .....arr.	mrn	5 43	6 18		6 47	mrn	....	8 8		8 18	8 32	....	8 55	....	....	9 10	9 29		9 53		....	1032	....	....	....	1123		....	....	1231	1 24
—	**Accrington**........dep.	5 7	....	....		Through Train, Bradford	6 51	....	Through Train, Blackpool		....	....	....	9 0	....	....	....	9 36		1022		....	....	....	....	....	....		1152	Via Padiham.	1256	1 40
42¼	Huncoat	5 11	....	....			6 55	....			....	....	....	9 4	....	....	....	9 40		....		....	....	....	....	....	....		1156		1 0	1 44
43½	Hapton	5 15	....	....			6 59	....			....	....	....	9 8	....	....	....	9 44		....		....	....	....	....	....	....		12 0		1 4	1 48
45	Rose Grove **783**	5 19	....	....	6 51		7 3	....		8 23	....	....	8 50	9 12	....	....	....	9 50	10 2	....		....	....	....	....	....	....	1143	12 5		1 8	1 52
46	Burnley Barracks.......	5 24	....	....	6 54		7 7	....		8 26	....	....	8 53	9 16	....	....	....	9 53	10 5	a		....	....	....	....	....	....	1146	12 8		1 12	1 56
46¾	**Burnley** (Bank Top)....	5 26	....	....	7 0		7 9	....		8 29	....	....	8 55	9 18	....	....	....	9 55	10 7	1033	1022	....	....	....	....	....	....	1150	1210		1 14	1 58
48¼	Brierfield	5 35	....	....	7a12		7 23	....		8 36	....	....	9 2	9 26	....	....	....	10 3	....	1042	⌐	....	....	....	....	....	....	1156	1218		1 22	2 7
50	Nelson	5 38	....	....	7a16		7 26	....		8 39	....	....	9 6	9 30	....	....	....	10 6	....	1045	....	....	....	....	....	....	....	1159	1221		1 25	2 10
52	**Colne 631** ....(**637** arr.	5 46	....	....	7a22		7 36	....		8 47	....	....	9 13	9 37	....	....	....	1014	....	1052	....	....	....	....	....	....	....	12 6	1230		1 34	2 28
63¼	**Skipton 624, 627,** "	6 25	....	....	....		8 14	mrn		9 23	....	....	....	....	....	....	....	1041	....	1128	....	....	....	....	....	....	....	1242	1843		2a15	2 56

Extract from *Bradshaw*, October 1911, showing part of the Liverpool, Southport, Blackpool, Preston, Accrington, Burnley, Colne and Todmorden (L&Y) service.

opened on 17th August 1848. It met with the line from Blackburn that had opened in June that same year. Accrington to Burnley Bank Top followed on 1st December, and finally Colne was reached on 1st February 1849.

The Leeds and Bradford Extension Railway (L&BER) had been working towards Colne from the Skipton direction. Prior to either company reaching the town there was an agreement in 1847 that they would share the station there. Because of the delays on the ELR route the L&BER arrived in town first, opening the line from Skipton in October 1848, some five months before the ELR arrived to create the through route. The first engine shed in Colne was a two-road structure, opened by the L&BER on 20th October 1848. The agreement to share the station with the ELR extended to that company also servicing and turning its engines at the L&BER shed.

With the coming of the Leeds and Liverpool Canal, Barnoldswick had grown from a rural village to a small town with several cotton mills. It featured in abortive proposals to be part of a through route from Gisburn (on the Blackburn to Hellifield route) to Earby as early as 1846, but when it became clear that these would not materialise local businessmen formed the Barnoldswick Railway Company to construct their own branch line, albeit the station at Barnoldswick was built as a through line, perhaps in the vain hope that the link to Gisburn would one day be built. The line was authorised by Parliament in 1865 and work started in 1867. Although it was a straight line less than two miles long, from Barnoldswick Junction near Earby, the branch had substantial earthworks and a bridge over the canal and took four years to complete. Barnoldswick trains were worked by the Midland Railway from the opening on 8th February 1871.

The last line to be constructed, by the mighty L&YR rather than a local company, was the loop from near Blackburn, through Great Harwood, Simonstone and Padiham to Rose Grove. It was described as the most expensive line, mile for mile, that the L&YR built and numerous civil engineering difficulties were encountered. There were cuttings, long embankments and viaducts on the route, which opened in 1877. To protect the viaduct and embankments at Martholme the railway company had to buy the rights to the coal underneath the route, and then leave it in the ground to prevent subsidence. As well as local traffic, it provided an alternative route for freight and through passenger trains avoiding the busy line through Accrington. Many excursion trains to Blackpool, from Yorkshire and East Lancashire, would be routed this way.

PASSENGER SERVICES

The main routes in this volume carried local and semi-fast services, including through coaches for London from Colne over the line to Bury continuing to Manchester and Stockport. At Colne, where the L&YR met the Midland, many services terminated but there were through workings from Manchester and East Lancashire to Skipton and beyond from the earliest days. Padiham Loop local trains operated between Blackburn and Rose Grove or Burnley, connecting with other services at both ends. The L&YR introduced railmotors between Burnley and Colne and opened three new halts to compete with local trams. Barnoldswick Branch trains mainly shuttled between there and Earby, although there were some through trains to Skipton.

In LMS days the pre-grouping locomotives were replaced on local passenger trains by new 2-6-4T engines that held sway until dieselisation. Summer excursions to the coastal resorts would be mainly handled by LMS Black 5s and Crab 2-6-0s but on busy days anything that could turn a wheel could be pressed into service. Local services were dieselised from the late 1950s, mainly operated by Cravens DMUs, but the excursions continued to be mainly steam hauled until this traffic ended.

Rise and fall – passenger closures

These lines were busy into BR days but then the inevitable decline began as mines and industry contracted, holiday habits changed and alternative transport became available.

Some intermediate stations closed before the lines themselves. The first was New Hall Bridge Halt, one of the three L&YR railmotor stops, which closed in 1948. Baxenden station closed to passengers in 1951 followed by lightly used and remote Elslack the following year. The railmotor halts at Reedley Hallows and Bott Lane closed in 1956.

Perhaps the first really significant closure was the local service on the Padiham Loop, where the last scheduled train ran on 30th November 1957. Simonstone closed completely to passengers but the line itself remained open and summer excursion trains continued to call at Great Harwood and Padiham for a further seven years. Local goods services were withdrawn in 1964 and the double track line became a single track short branch to Padiham Power Station from Rose Grove West Junction, a role that continued for nearly 30 more years.

Intermediate passenger station closures continued with Foulridge closing in 1959 and Haslingden the following year. Haslingden is a significant town but the station was remote from the centre, which was well served by frequent buses from Accrington to Rawtenstall, and it closed on 7th November 1960. As at Padiham, summer excursions continued to call at its platforms for a few more years.

Daily excursions from the East Lancashire towns, especially during the 'Wakes' or holiday weeks, were very popular running to Southport, Blackpool, Morecambe and the Lake District. There were also weekly long-distance holiday services, such as to Devon or the East Coast. Such were the numbers of trains that numerous carriage sidings and depots were needed to accommodate the stock. This would usually be non-corridor compartment coaches for the local excursions, and corridor coaches with lavatories for the longer distances. Colne had a large carriage depot of six covered sidings. After it had closed as an engine shed the turntable was retained so that locos arriving with or to collect coaches could be turned. The facilities were updated with a new staff accommodation block being opened in 1959 but from the early 1960s excursion and holiday traffic quickly declined and the depot closed in 1967.

Services to Barnoldswick had declined, perhaps with official encouragement, after 1955. That year the daily service dropped from 12 to two trains per day, but this continued until 1965, with goods services ceasing the following year.

Stubbins Junction to Accrington, part of the through route from Manchester and Bury to Colne and Skipton, closed completely from 5th December 1966, the same day as the line beyond Rawtenstall to Bacup. The intermediate station at Helmshore closed with the line.

The Colne to Skipton line closed in February 1970, along with the surviving intermediate stations at Thornton-in-Craven and Earby. This ended this through route between Lancashire and Yorkshire, and there have been campaigns ever since to reopen the line. Colne became the terminus of a single track branch and was soon de-staffed. Its buildings were demolished leaving just a small platform shelter, a situation basically unchanged over 50 years later.

DMU introduction

Local services between Blackburn, Colne and Skipton, and those coming from Manchester and Bury, were transformed from the late 1950s by the introduction of DMUs. Accrington shed closed to steam in 1961 and said goodbye to its LMS 2-6-4Ts that had handled so many of the local trains. It became a diesel servicing depot for the next 11 years, with an allocation of Cravens sets. Elsewhere in the country DMUs were often of the power car and trailer variety but with the steep gradients of this area, not least the fearsome Baxenden bank, the Cravens were twin power cars. They were also of two types. The first had two 150hp AEC engines under each car, later class 105. These had a long life and were associated with the East Lancashire services until withdrawn in the 1980s. The second Cravens type was introduced in 1960 and fitted with a single Rolls Royce 238hp engine under each car. They also had hydraulic transmission, later designated class 113. They could be distinguished from the 'standard' Cravens by the large four-character headcode boxes above the driver's cab. These sets were considered unreliable and several were written off after catching fire, all being withdrawn by 1969.

Last steam in 1968

Through the 1960s steam was in rapid decline around the country and some parts were completely dieselised quite early in the decade but the North West of England became the last area to use steam locomotives and Rose Grove, along with Carnforth and Lostock Hall, was one of the last steam sheds, working right up to August 1968. It became a place of pilgrimage for steam enthusiasts capturing the last few freight workings of grimy Black 5 and 8F locomotives.

1. Blackburn to Accrington

BLACKBURN

Blackburn station opened on 1st June 1846 with the B&PR. This extended eastwards to Accrington on 10th June 1848. There was a large goods shed and yard adjacent to the station. The station was rebuilt and expanded between 1885 and 1888 with the large trainshed a notable feature. With the retrenchment of services in the 1970s trains were concentrated on the main island platform. By that time trains were limited to the Preston to Colne and Blackburn to Manchester DMU services with some freight services. The goods shed by the station closed in 1973 but that at Bolton Road remained in railway use until around 2010. Later, trains were reintroduced over the Copy Pit line to West Yorkshire, and the Ribble Valley line to Clitheroe and Blackburn became much busier again. The trainshed however was deteriorating and in 2000 was dismantled with new buildings installed on the main island platform, still accessed by subway from Blackburn Boulevard. Thirty or so years after it fell into disuse, Platform 4, on its separate island was also refurbished and returned to service.

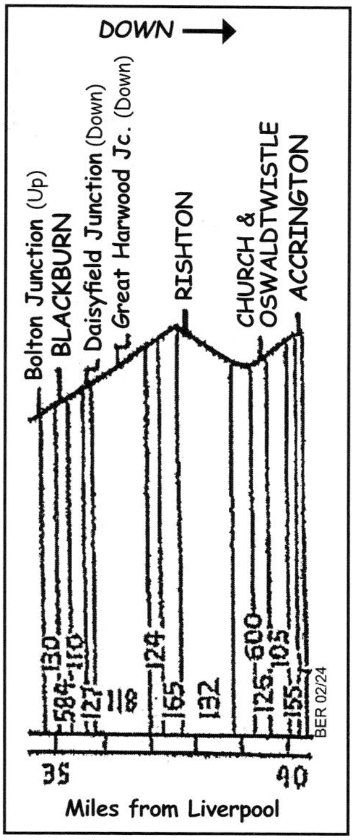

1. Stanier Jubilee 6P5F 4-6-0 no. 45565 *Victoria* with 1N55, a Saturdays Only Blackpool to Bradford Exchange service, passing Blackburn West signal box on 6th August 1966. Note the gantry of semaphore signals behind the train. Blackburn West, and most of the other mechanical boxes on the East Lancashire route, closed when Preston Power Box was commissioned in 1972. 45565, a Low Moor loco at this time, was withdrawn on 6th January 1967. (M.Chapman courtesy ColourRail.co.uk)

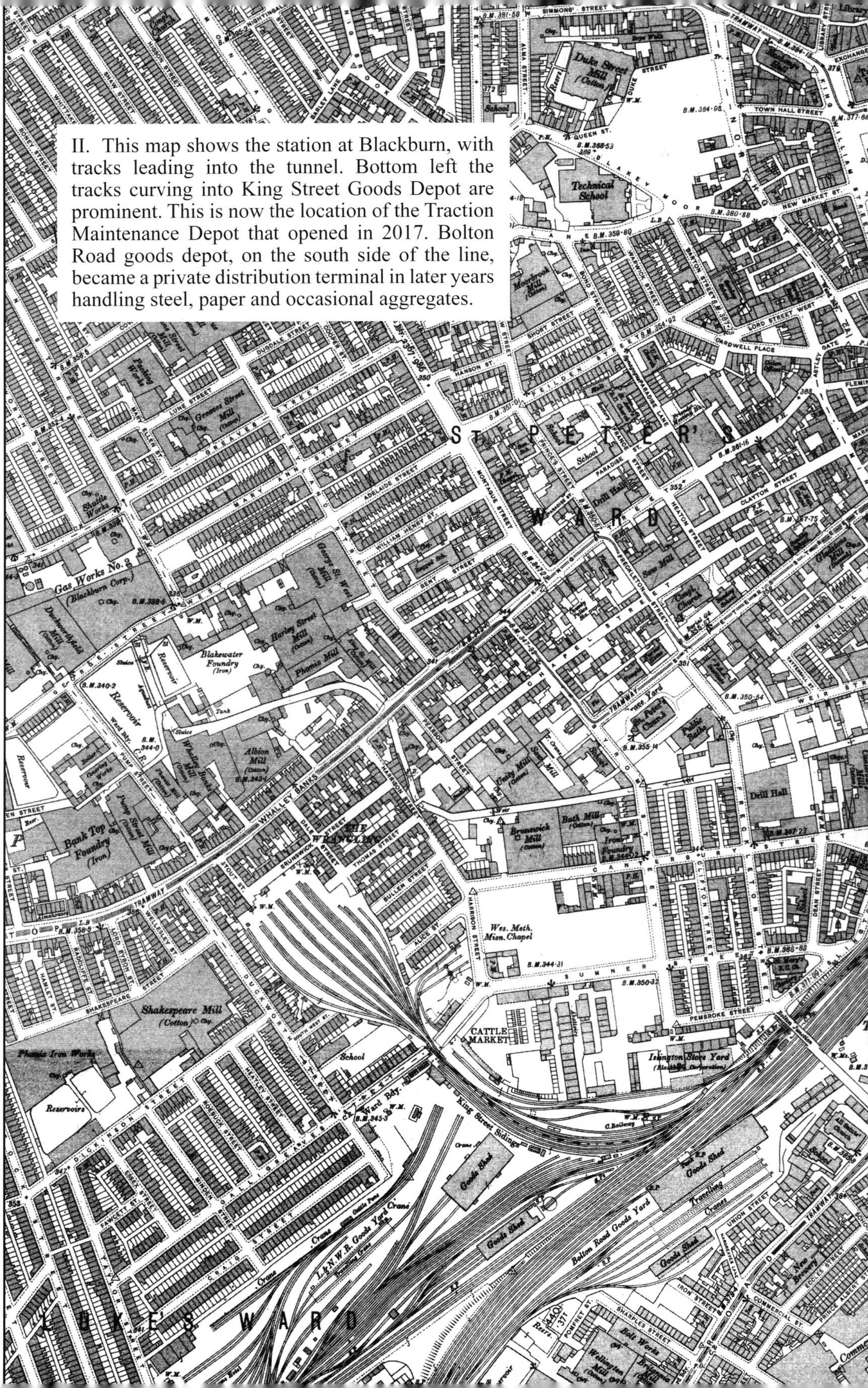

II. This map shows the station at Blackburn, with tracks leading into the tunnel. Bottom left the tracks curving into King Street Goods Depot are prominent. This is now the location of the Traction Maintenance Depot that opened in 2017. Bolton Road goods depot, on the south side of the line, became a private distribution terminal in later years handling steel, paper and occasional aggregates.

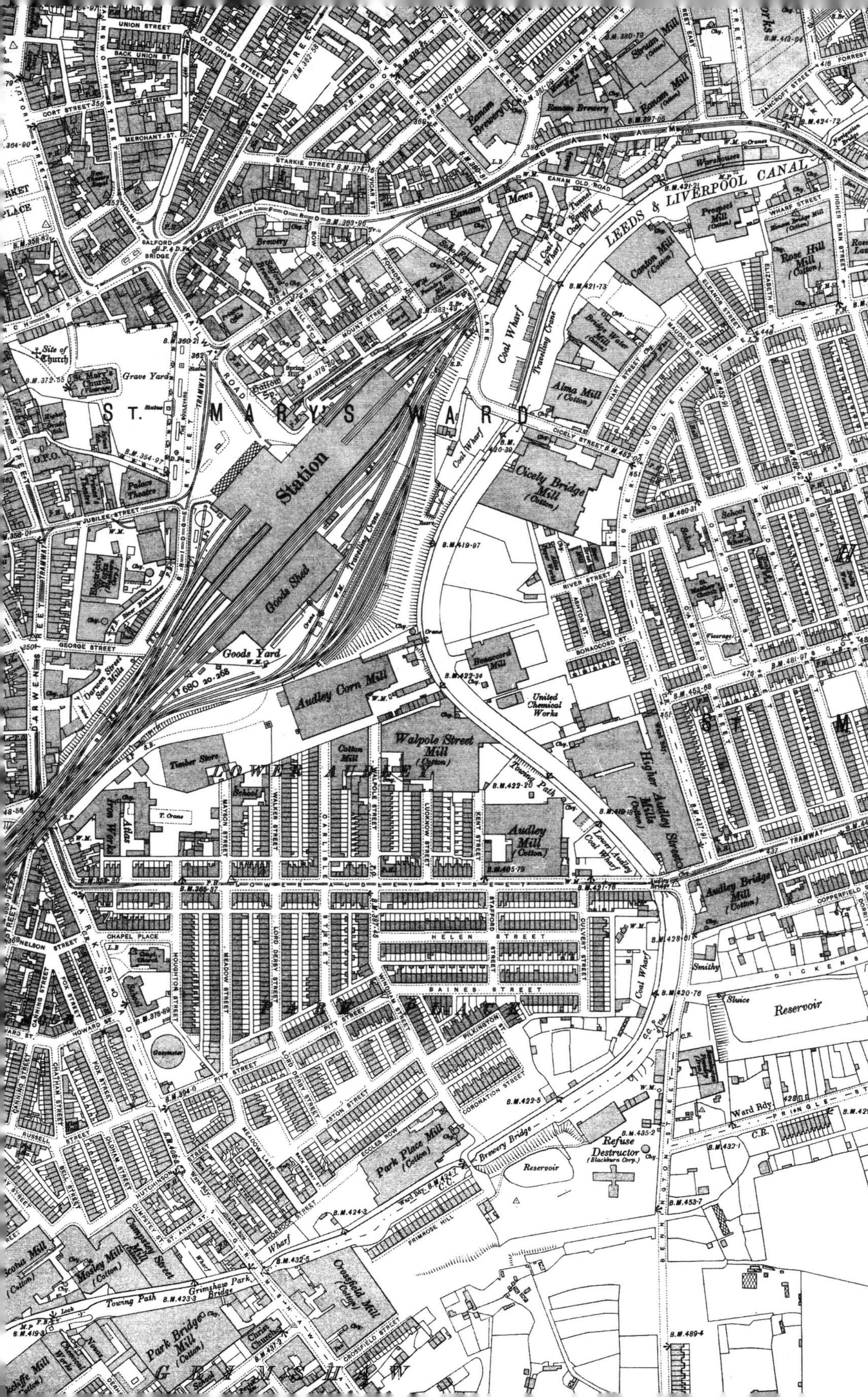

UNION STREET
BACK UNION ST.
OLD CHAPEL STREET
CORT STREET
MERCHANT ST.
PENNY STREET
STARKIE STREET
VICAR ST.
Eanam Brewery
Eanam Brewery
Eanam Mill (Cotton)
Stream Mill (Cotton)
QUARRY ST.
FORREST
BANCROFT STREET
Warehouses
EANAM OLD ROAD
LEEDS & LIVERPOOL CANAL
WHARF STREET
HIGHER BARN STREET
Prospect Mill (Cotton)
Rose Hill Mill (Cotton)
ELIZABETH ST.
Eanam Mews
Brewery
BOW ST.
FOUNDRY HILL
Tunnel
Coal Wharf
Canton Mill (Cotton)
Bridge Water Mill (Cotton)
Alma Mill (Cotton)
Travelling Crane
MAUDSLEY ST.
HART STREET
BALFORD BRIDGE
MOUNT STREET
Spring Hill
Site of Church
St. Mary's Church (Vicarage)
Grave Yard
ST. MARY'S WARD
TRAMWAY
Statue
CICELY LANE
CICELY STREET
Cicely Bridge Mill (Cotton)
Station
G.P.O.
Palace Theatre
Prince's Theatre
JUBILEE STREET
Electricity Works
Goods Shed
Travelling Crane
Goods Yard
GEORGE STREET
DARWEN STREET
Darwen Street Saw Mills
RIVER STREET
ASHTON ST.
BONACCORD ST.
Bonaccord Mill
School
St. Matthew's Church
Vicarage
Audley Corn Mill
United Chemical Works
Walpole Street Mill (Cotton)
Cotton Mill
Timber Store
LOWER AUDLEY
Towing Path
Higher Audley Mills (Cotton)
Higher Audley Street
Atlas Iron Works
T. Crane
WALKER STREET
MAYSON STREET
WALPOLE STREET
LUCKNOW STREET
KENT STREET
Audley Mill (Cotton)
Lower Audley Coal Wharf
Audley Bridge
Audley Bridge Mill (Cotton)
TRAMWAY
COPPERFIELD ST.
CHAPEL PLACE
NELSON STREET
LORD DERBY STREET
MEADOW STREET
HOUGHTON STREET
STAFFORD STREET
HELEN STREET
BAINES STREET
QUEVERT STREET
Coal Wharf
Smithy
DICKENS
Sluice
Reservoir
PARK ROAD
FOX STREET
CANNING STREET
HOWARD ST.
PILKINGTON ST.
PITT STREET
Gasometer
CORONATION STREET
ASTON STREET
ECCLES ROW
Park Place Mill (Cotton)
Brewery Bridge
Refuse Destructor (Blackburn Corpn.)
Reservoir
Ward Bdy.
PRINGLE ST.
BENNINGTON STREET
CHATHAM STREET
RUSSELL STREET
OLDHAM STREET
BELL STREET
HUTCHINSON ST.
ST. ANNS ST.
PRIMROSE HILL
Wharf
Mosley Mill (Cotton)
Cemetery Street Mill
Grimshaw Park Bridge
Towing Path
Lock
Crossfield Mill (Cotton)
CROSSFIELD STREET
Park Bridge Mill (Cotton)
Christ Church
School
GRIMSHAW

King Street Goods Depot, Coal Depot and Traction Maintenance Depot

King Street, to the west of the passenger station, was the East Lancashire Railway goods yard in Blackburn and operated from 1848 to 1969 when it became a coal concentration depot (CCD). Access was from Blackburn Bolton Junction, where the line to Darwen and Bolton also diverges.

2. The CCD used an ex-BR Drewry class 04 0-6-0DM shunter no. D2272 *Alfie*, previously based at Bradford Hammerton Street Depot, seen here on 3rd September 1988. In its early years in Blackburn it sported a black livery. The facility closed in 1995 and the shunter was later preserved by the Heritage Shunter Trust at Rowsley in Derbyshire. The yard lay empty for many years but on 26th October 2017 Northern Rail opened King Street Traction Maintenance Depot on the site. The coal handling facilities have been cleared and there is now a six-road facility for cleaning, servicing and refuelling DMUs from Northern's fleet. (Gordon Edgar)

3. Northern Sprinter no. 150139 heads west from Blackburn with a Colne to Blackpool South stopping service on 23rd March 2017. This vantage point from Wainwright Bridge was not available to photographers in steam days but it shows the limited running lines and sidings that remain at Blackburn with the modernised station beyond. The line into the maintenance depot diverges under the bridge. (Mark Bartlett)

4. The main station building at Blackburn in 1908, seen from the Boulevard, with early tramcars also in view. The railway is elevated here and the platforms accessed by ramps from ground level. The long canopy, which survives today, allowed passengers to alight from cabs and parcels office staff to load and unload carts under cover. The trainshed looms large behind the building, and would do so until its demolition in 2000. Today, Blackburn's buses still operate from the bus station outside the railway station entrance. (Lancashire & Yorkshire Railway Society)

5. The 13.10 Colne to Preston Sunday service, formed of a Cravens class 105 DMU, waits departure time at an otherwise deserted Blackburn station on 2nd April 1975. This was probably the low point for passenger services, with just an hourly stopping train on the Colne to Preston route and similar intervals from here to Bolton and Manchester Victoria. These services were concentrated on this island platform and that to the right only saw occasional use. The huge trainshed would witness the resurgence in services before it was demolished in 2000. Picture no. 7 was taken from a similar position almost 40 years later. (Tom Heavyside)

087

ervices
2
Gentlemen
Waiting room
4

← 6. BR class 56 Co-Co no. 56087 uses the Goods Loop passing the lofty trainshed at Blackburn on 11th February 1997. Passenger services between Lancashire and Yorkshire via the Copy Pit route had been reintroduced on a limited basis in 1984 but by the 1990s had grown to an hourly service, which has continued to the present day. The old station however only had another three years' service before the major rebuild. This lengthy train is 6E41, an EWS Enterprise service from Warrington Arpley to Lackenby that mainly comprised empty steel carriers from Gilbraith's at Blackburn. It will run through Blackburn Tunnel on the up line before crossing to the Down East Lancs at Daisyfield Junction. (Paul D. Shannon)

↙ 7. Pacer no. 142041 calls at Blackburn's reinstated platform 4 with a Colne to Preston service on 14th February 2018. The much maligned four-wheeled Pacers were the most frequently used units on Colne services for many years with four sets being needed to maintain an hourly service between Blackpool South and Colne. A typical East Lancashire line diagram would see these units cover almost 500 miles, with around 250 station stops, each day. Picture no. 5 was taken from a similar position over 40 years earlier when platform 4 was not used. (Mark Bartlett)

Blackburn Tunnel

8. Immediately east of the station is the 435 yards long Blackburn Tunnel. It has two tracks, but with modern signalling these are both bi-directional lines. Blackburn East signal box stood near the west portal. In this view from around 1962 a 2-6-4T can be seen in the bay platform with a passenger train, probably heading for Clitheroe and Hellifield. That service was withdrawn on 10th September 1962 and these platforms were later cut back, as seen in picture no. 6. When trains to Clitheroe were reinstated in 1994 they ran through from Manchester Victoria and Bolton rather than starting here. (Peter Fidczuk collection)

Further views of Blackburn can be seen in
Blackburn to Hellifield (the Ribble Valley Line).

Daisyfield Junction

III. Daisyfield Junction, to the east of Blackburn Tunnel, came into being when the BBC&WRR line to Clitheroe opened on 22nd June 1850. This map extract shows local rail served factories. Daisyfield Goods Yard, accessed from the East Lancashire line, lies in the 'V' of the junction adjacent to the passenger station. This is on the Clitheroe line but closed on 3rd November 1958, four years before the withdrawal of local trains. It did not reopen when services resumed in 1994.

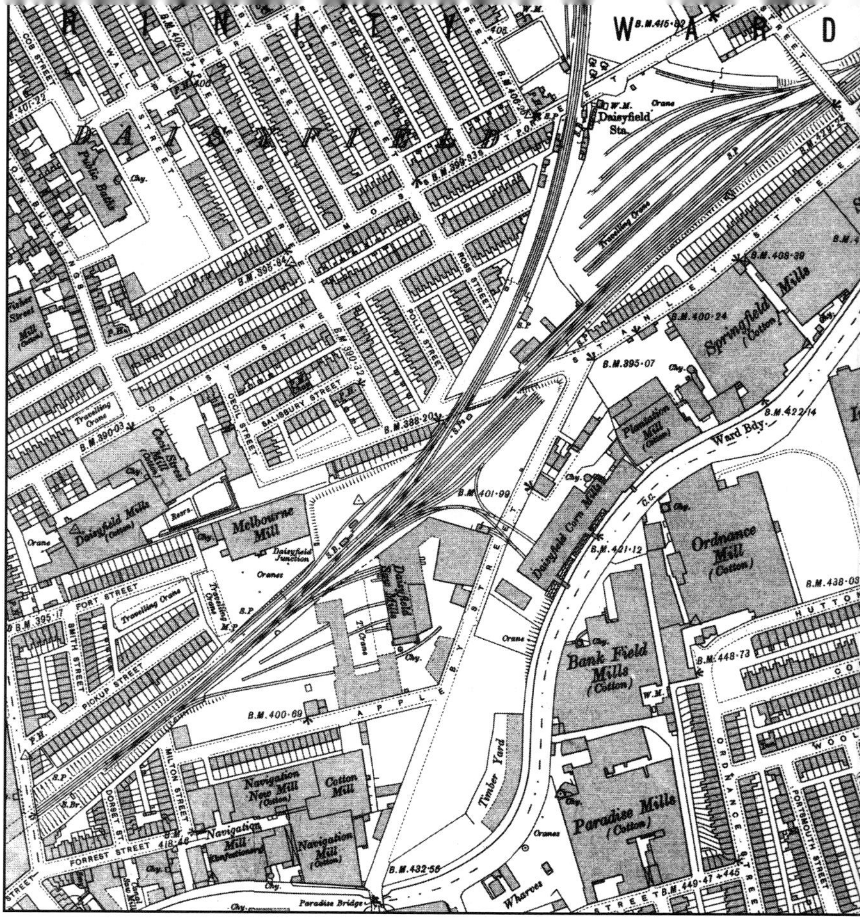

9. This view, from above the east portal of Blackburn Tunnel, shows the signals controlling Daisyfield Junction which lies immediately beyond them. Northern Sprinter no. 150108 is heading towards Accrington, with a service for Manchester and Rainford via the Copy Pit line on 13th September 2023. The trees on the right conceal the modern commercial premises that have been built where the rail served mills once stood. There are signals for both running lines as they are bi-directional through the tunnel and as far as the junction. (Mark Bartlett)

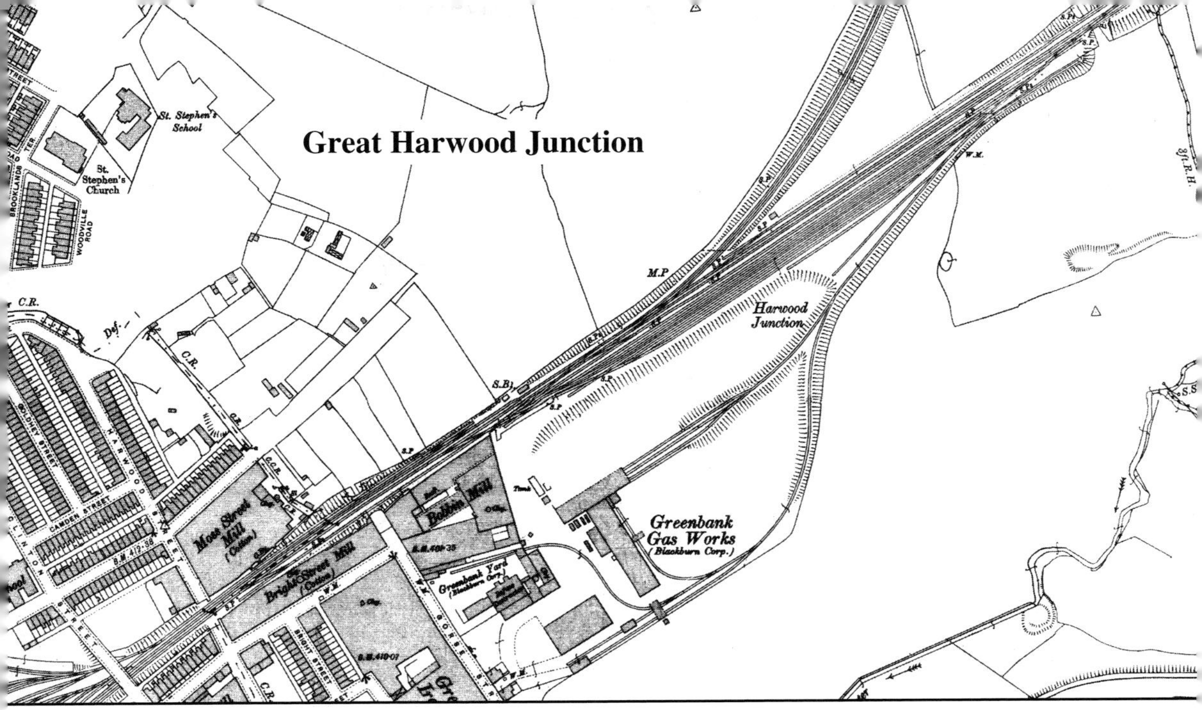

IV. An L&YR signal box on the north side of the line controlled Great Harwood Junction, which opened with the Padiham Loop Line in 1877. The last through trains ran over the loop on 30th November 1964. Blackburn Gas Works at Greenbank was also rail served. Almost every piece of open land in this map extract has since been built on, mainly with business parks.

10. Such is the level of building, and growth of trees, at the site of Great Harwood Junction that no remains can be seen from passing trains today. This was the scene in 1966 as Stanier Black 5 4-6-0 no. 45107 passes heading an excursion towards Accrington. This was around two years after trains last used the Padiham Loop but the box is still controlling the main line. To the left is Blackburn Gas Works, which in the 1960s changed from producing coal gas to being a natural gas storage site until 2002. The signal box closed before the Preston Power Box resignalling. (ColourRail.co.uk)

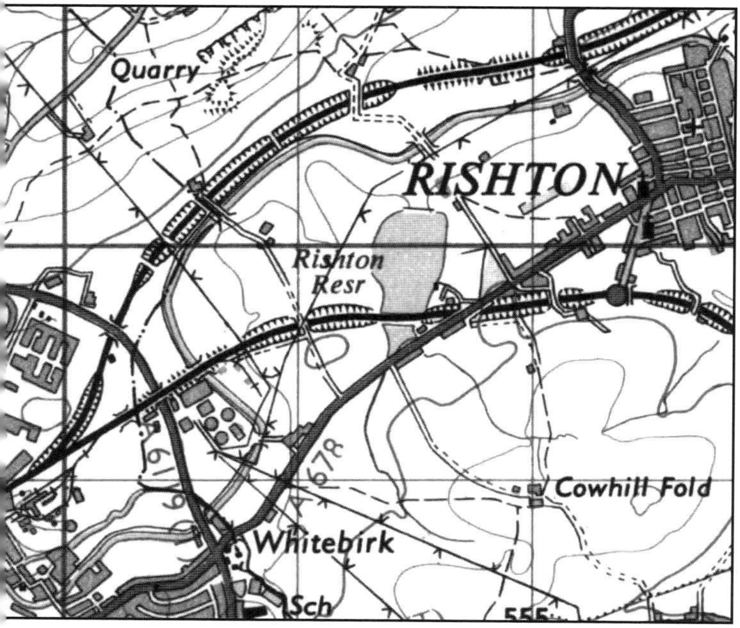

Whitebirk Power Station

V. Just to the east of Great Harwood Junction was Whitebirk Power Station, which opened in 1921 to the south of the line and the west of the Leeds and Liverpool canal, which was initially used to deliver coal from the Burnley Coalfield. The canal allows wide-beam boats and there are no locks between Blackburn and Burnley. Continuing eastwards the railway crosses the canal and Rishton reservoir before passing under the A678 road and reaching Rishton station. (1955 OS 7th Series 1in to 1 mile map extract.)

11. A Northern class 195 CAF DMU crosses the Leeds and Liverpool Canal at Whitebirk with a York to Blackpool North service, on 22nd December 2022. When the power station expanded, sidings opened around 1942 and a new concrete signal box was provided. This closed when Preston Power Box took control of this route in 1973. The railway coal handling facilities were built on the east side of the canal, connected by overhead conveyors from the stockpiles. British Waterways' barges continued to supply the station, as well as coal trains from Yorkshire, but it closed in 1976. The concrete wharves where the barges were unloaded can be seen on the right of this picture. A retail park now occupies the power station site. (Mark Bartlett)

Rishton Tunnel

12. East from Whitebirk the line crosses Rishton Reservoir on a causeway. Nearby Rishton Tunnel, at a mere 68 yards, is more of a long bridge carrying the main road to Blackburn. Rishton's first station opened here in June 1848 but this should be considered a temporary facility as it moved to the present site, much nearer the village, around 1852-53. This view looks towards Blackburn from the pavement by the west portal. Sprinter no. 150135, on a Preston to Colne stopping service, has just crossed the reservoir as it approaches the tunnel. (Mark Bartlett)

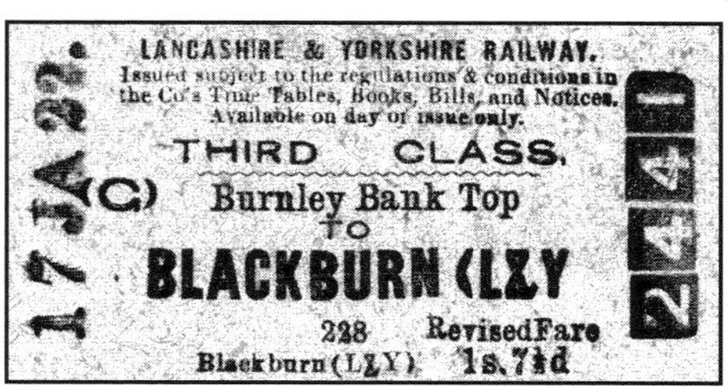

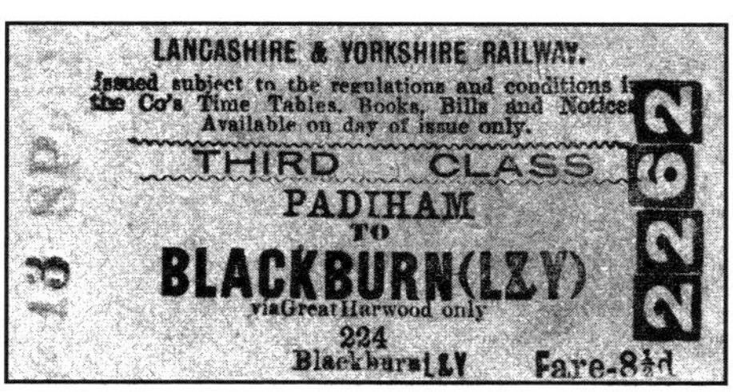

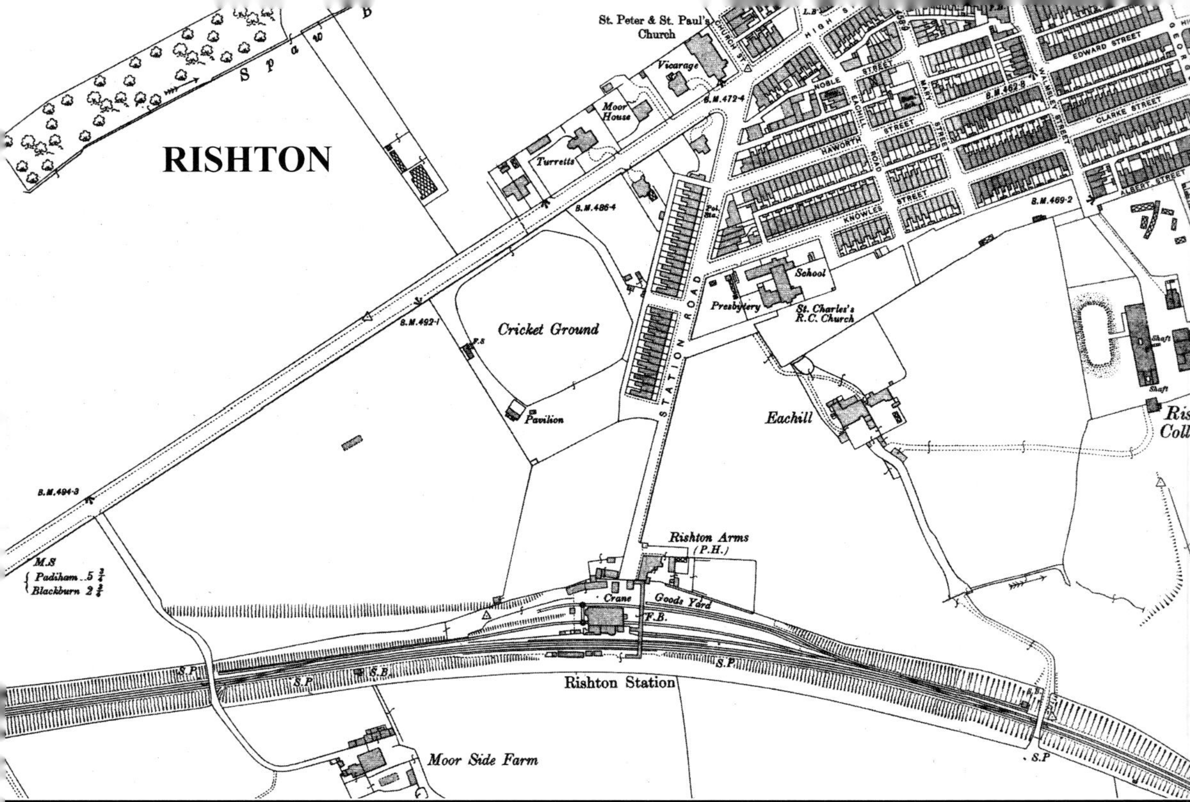

VI. Rishton had a substantial goods yard, and a long footbridge spanning the goods yard tracks from a remote ticket office by the yard entrance. The footbridge became partly redundant and was cut back after the last pick-up goods train left in November 1968.

13. Rishton, looking east, in L&YR days. The stone station building was distinctive as other stations east of Blackburn tended to be built from brick, or brick and timber. It was combined with the goods shed into a single building. The footbridge at this time was fully enclosed. (John Alsop collection)

14. Stanier 8F 2-8-0 no. 48618 heads east through Rishton with a rake of unfitted 16T mineral empties on 5th November 1966. These were probably returning from either Wyre Dock power station or nearby Whitebirk to a Yorkshire colliery. Coal trains were previously handled by WD 2-8-0s but displaced 8Fs arrived in the mid-1960s to replace them. The stone goods shed, which would close two years later, appears to have steel bracing supporting the end wall and the footbridge roof has been removed revealing the open lattice steelwork, although still at its full length at this time. (G.M. Wilkinson courtesy ColourRail.co.uk)

15. CAF 3-car DMU no. 195131 speeds through Rishton heading to Blackpool North from York on 18th May 2022. Only Colne services call at Rishton, but the unstaffed station is still reasonably busy. In 2019-20 the official passenger figures were 45,082. The footbridge now just spans the running lines and platforms. Behind the trees the old goods yard is occupied by a car park and housing. (Mark Bartlett)

Between Rishton and Church & Oswaldtwistle

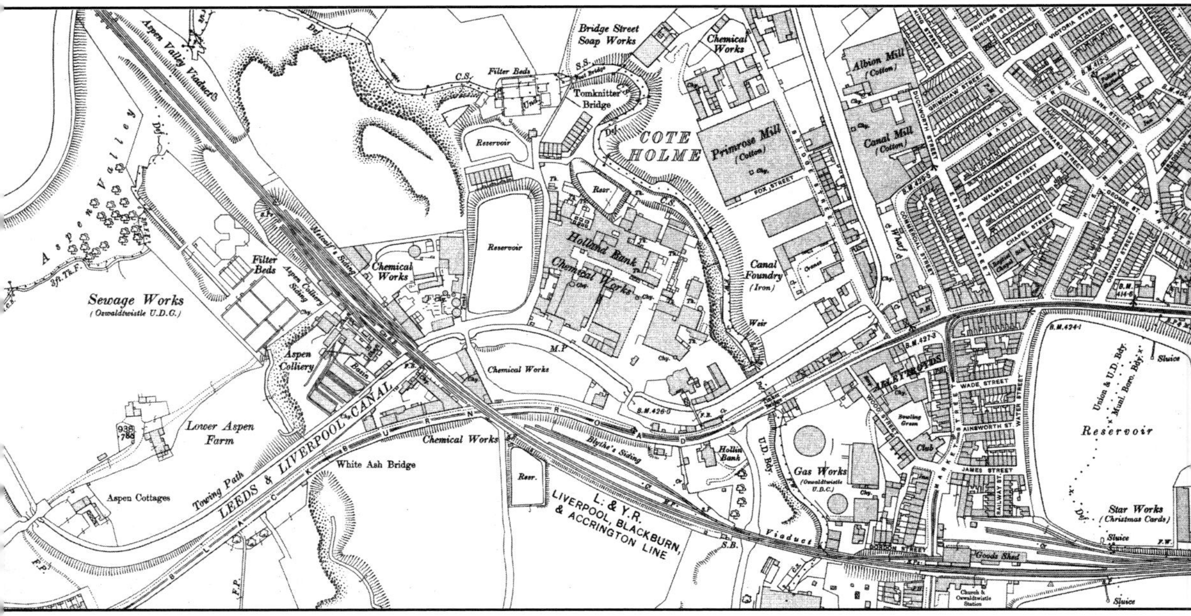

VII. Map extract of the line to the west of Church showing the Aspen Valley Viaduct before it was filled in, the 'U' shaped course of the Leeds and Liverpool Canal, Aspen Colliery and, bottom right, Church & Oswaldtwistle station.

16. Just to the east of Rishton the line crosses the M65 motorway on a large bridge opened in 1984. Another new bridge, slightly below it, carries the slightly diverted Leeds and Liverpool canal over the M65. This view from the towpath on the canal bridge shows Northern Sprinter no. 156461 crossing the motorway, with a Colne to Preston stopping service, on 5th September 2022. (Mark Bartlett)

17. Nearing Church & Oswaldtwistle the line crosses the canal twice as it follows the contour around the Aspen Valley. The railway takes a much straighter route on an embankment, which hides an interesting structure. When built in 1848 it crossed this valley on a timber trestle viaduct, comprising 33 spans, each 25ft across and reaching a maximum height of 70ft above the valley floor. In L&YR days, to reduce the risk of fire and to save on maintaining this huge structure, it was gradually buried, once the stream had been culverted, by tipping mine waste. The main image, looking northwards, shows some evidence of that embankment construction from tipped spoil. The smaller image shows infilling operations taking place, with spoil being hand-shovelled from wagons headed by an L&YR 2-4-2T. This long process was finally completed in 1925 and there is now no trace of the magnificent bridge. (Lancashire and Yorkshire Railway Society).

↓ 18. Sprinter no. 150120 has just left Church & Oswaldtwistle with a Colne to Preston service on 5th September 2022 and is crossing the Leeds and Liverpool Canal. On the left here are the remains of Aspen Colliery, served by rail and canal but closed in 1922 although several large coke ovens are still on the site and are scheduled as an ancient monument, along with the adjacent canal basin. The Sprinter is approaching the embankment that replaced Aspen timber viaduct. (Mark Bartlett)

CHURCH & OSWALDTWISTLE

19. Church station opened on 17th June 1848 but from 1st July 1895 it was known as Church & Oswaldtwistle. It occupies an elevated position and Market Street passes under the line by the entrance. It had a goods yard on the north side, which closed in 1966, although a nearby yard, shown as Blythe's Siding on Map VII, handled scrap traffic until 1981. After the station became unstaffed the platform buildings were demolished and now there are just the usual Northern shelters on each side. This view looks towards Rishton and was probably taken in early BR days but before the LMR enamel signs were installed. (John Alsop collection)

20. Looking north on Market Street, this is the main entrance to Church & Oswaldtwistle station in L&YR days. Two horse-drawn carts are passing the scene but there is also a single electrified tram line and an early motorcar parked by the roadside. The ground floor canopy marks the entrance to a slightly higher level passageway under the tracks, affording access to platform staircases. The elevated passageway is still there today, as are the stairs. (Lens of Sutton Association)

Accrington Shed

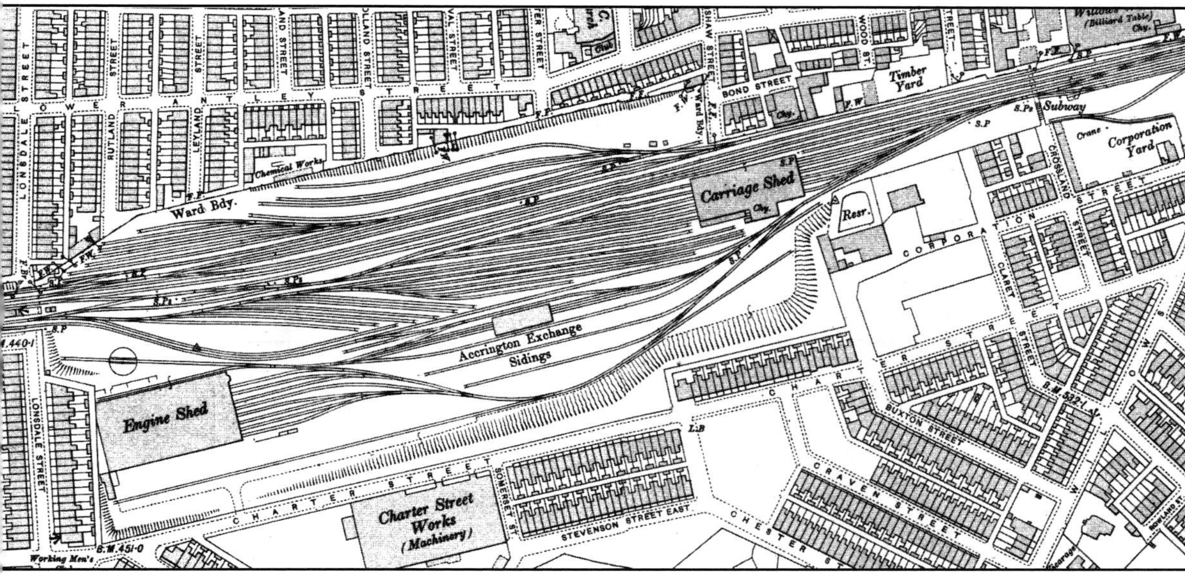

VIII. Accrington Shed and its associated sidings occupied most of the south side of the line between Church & Oswaldtwistle and Accrington stations. This 25ins to 1 mile map extract shows the shed layout around 1913, with eight covered roads and the carriage depot (previous 1873 loco shed) to the right.

21. The first shed at Accrington was a two road building opened by the ELR on 1st June 1848, alongside the station, and closed in 1873. It was replaced by a new L&YR built six road shed on the south side of the line between Accrington and Church & Oswaldtwistle. This only lasted until 1899, when it was closed and converted into a carriage shed in 1904. The eight road shed shown here opened in 1899, further west than its predecessor. This is an LMS era view, with an L&YR 0-6-0 and two L&YR 2-4-2Ts visible along with a 'Crab' 2-6-0 and a LMS Fowler 4P 2-6-4T. (John Alsop collection)

22. The LMS rebuilt Accrington shed in 1937, reducing the covered area to six roads but providing a mechanical coaling plant. The changed roof design can be seen on 21st May 1960, although the office block alongside appears unchanged. A Cravens DMU and a Stanier 4MT 2-6-4T are on the two roads now outside and two more 2-6-4Ts, staple local passenger power for many years, can be seen in front of the main shed. Accrington closed to steam on 6th March 1961 but remained in use for DMU servicing until 1st October 1972 after which the DMUs were transferred to Newton Heath and the shed was demolished. (ColourRail.co.uk)

← *The Ian Allan Locomotive Shed Directory of 1961 described Accrington shed as a 10 minute walk from Church & Oswaldtwistle station but 15 minutes from Accrington. At that time it was coded 24A, as the main shed in a district that ranged from Skipton and Hellifield to Blackpool, Lancaster and Carnforth. 1961 however was when the shed closed to steam and in 1963 it was recoded as 10E while Carnforth became 10A, the district lead depot.*

23. This grainy picture was found, with its inscription, under the glass plate on top of a DMU engineer's desk at Derby around 1970. It appears to be a photocopy poking fun at Newton Heath depot but unfortunately the original has not been traced. The DMU is believed to be no. M51770 at Accrington in 1964.

(continued overleaf)

This Cravens class 113 Driving Motor Composite was one of the Rolls Royce engined cars with hydraulic transmission and on 14th March 1964 it was climbing Baxenden Bank on the 7.58am Skipton to Manchester Victoria train (8.42am from Accrington) when it failed and came to a stand at Shoe Mill. There were only two passengers on board but one noticed that the coach was on fire under the floor and alerted the driver. The passengers detrained and as Shoe Mill box was closed by this date the guard went back down to Accrington South to summon the fire brigade. Meanwhile the driver managed to separate the Driving Motor Brake Second no. M51745 and roll it a little way down the hill on the handbrake thereby saving this vehicle and the mail on board. The remote location, and lack of direct water supply, meant that M51770 could not be saved and the picture shows the result. The cause of the fire was the cardan shaft breaking and puncturing the fuel tank, which was on top of it in the form of a saddle, clearly a poor design feature which caused other fires and, despite modifications, led to the class 113 units all being withdrawn by 1969. M51770 was taken to Doncaster works and cut up in May 1964.
(Mick Boot courtesy of Railcar.co.uk)

ACCRINGTON

IX. Accrington station opened on 17th June 1848 as the line from Blackburn arrived in the town. The railway from Bury followed shortly after on 17th August and then the line to Burnley opened on 1st December. There were platforms on two sides of the triangle with a South to West curve for goods traffic and excursions. General goods facilities were at Scaitcliffe Street, alongside that curve, but these closed on 4th December 1967. There was also a Coal Depot known as Eagle Street, alongside the main passenger station entrance, and this closed on 5th October 1964. The line running south from Accrington crosses a mill reservoir, known as a lodge in Lancashire, on a viaduct as it immediately starts the climb of Baxenden Bank.

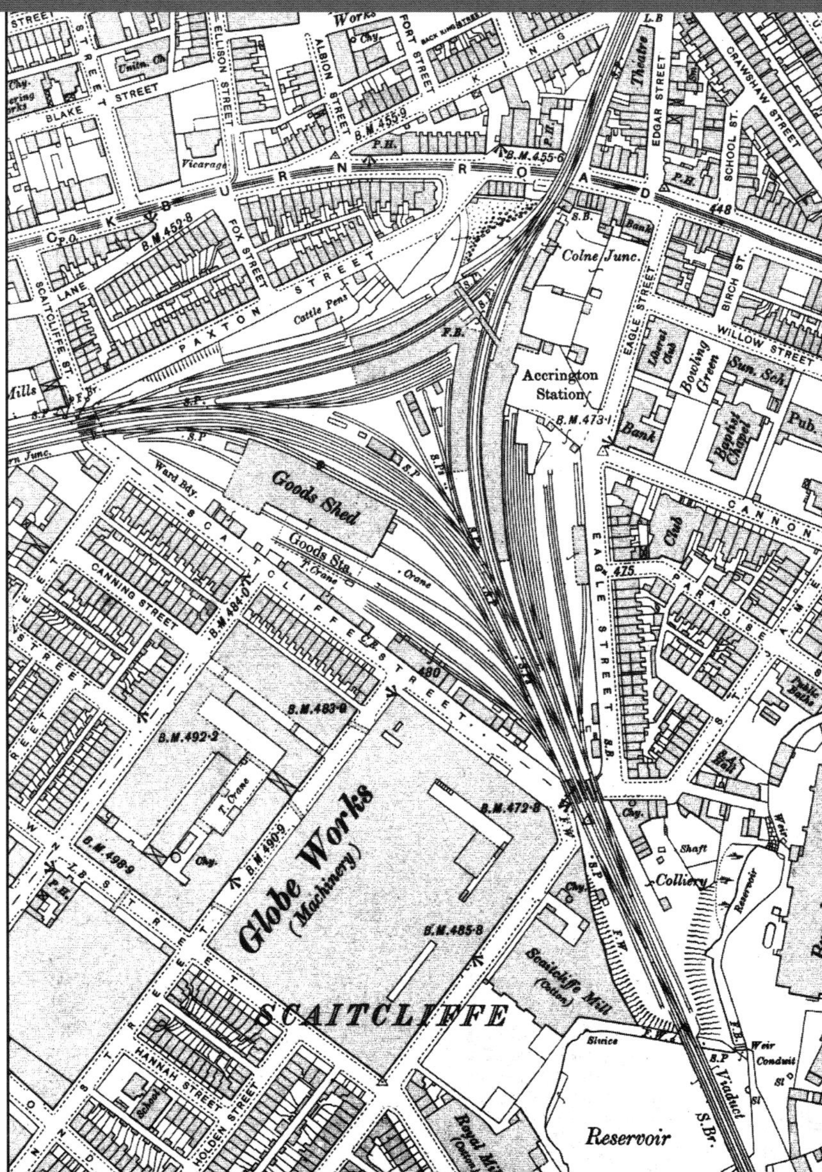

24. Accrington was where the line from Bury and Stubbins Junction met that from Preston and Blackburn and then continued towards Burnley and Colne. This view from L&YR days looks back along the Blackburn bound platform to the junction where, under the footbridge, some of the old East Lancashire Railway buildings on the low section of the Bury platform can be seen. At this time the footbridge was covered and spanned four tracks. (Lens of Sutton Association)

25. Accrington is viewed from the Bury platform on a wet 5th May 1963 with an engine driver in grease top cap making his way along the platform. At this time the station still had its full complement of ELR and L&YR buildings but that would soon change. After the 1966 closure of the Bury line the majority of buildings were swept away. Those on the Bury platform lingered a little longer for parcels traffic. After 1966 the footbridge would lose its roof and be cut back to just link the Blackburn and Burnley platforms. A small ticket office on the Burnley platform was constructed and served the station until a new building was constructed in 2010.
(Lens of Sutton Association/John Faulkner collection)

26. A view across the south to west curve at Accrington, towards the goods depot at Scaitcliffe Street, in 1965. Shorn of its *Bermuda* nameplates and looking very run down, Jubilee 4-6-0 no. 45600 is shunting a couple of wagons, while a Fowler 3F 'Jinty' 0-6-0T waits near the South Junction bracket signal, at the foot of Baxenden Bank. In diesel days, whenever rail head conditions were less than perfect, the first DMU of the day would usually be banked by the goods depot Jinty up the hill to Baxenden. 45600 was withdrawn from Newton Heath in December that year and cut up at Cashmore's, Great Bridge, the following April. There were no passenger platforms on this curve, which was only used by goods and excursion traffic. All railway features in this scene have since disappeared. (The late David Dyson courtesy Mike Taylor)

27. Looking towards Blackburn from the Accrington footbridge. To this day the check-railed curve through the platforms has a 10mph speed restriction. On 3rd May 1988, Pacers and Sprinters were fairly recent replacements for the 1st Generation DMUs. Pacer no. 142062 is on the 13.14 Colne to Preston while Sprinter no. 150201 is on the 12.45 Blackpool North to Leeds service. The ticket office building is now on the Burnley platform but the overall lack of waiting facilities compared to earlier years is very noticeable. The modern buildings above the two trains are on the alignment of the south to west curve. (Tom Heavyside)

28. For years intending passengers at Accrington had to use a steep path to reach the ticket office on the Burnley platform, and then cross the footbridge if travelling westwards. That changed in 2010 when a new ticket office, with ramped access, was opened on the site of the Bury line trackbed, back where the original booking office and other facilities had been until their demolition around 40 years earlier. This is the stylish eco-structure on New Year's Day 2011, soon after it opened. Community Rail Lancashire, which coordinates and supports the five community railways in the county, have their office in the basement of the building. In 2023 it was announced that a new footbridge with lifts will at long last be built to complement the modern office. (Mark Bartlett)

2. Stubbins Junction to Accrington

➔ *Gradient profile.*

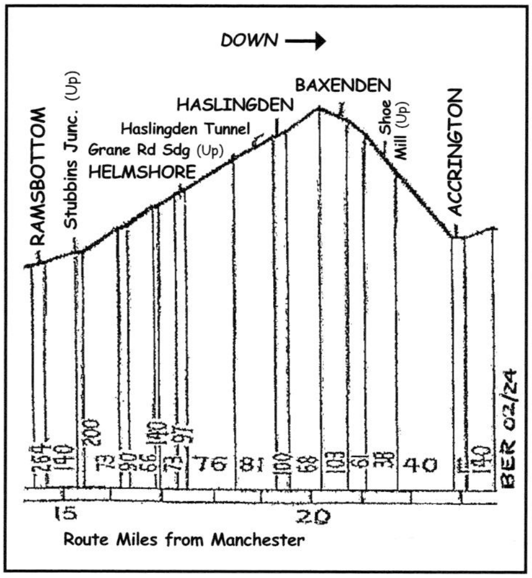

This section was always known locally as the Stubbins Junction to Accrington line. Ramsbottom, which is south of the junction, is covered in *Manchester to Bacup*.

➘ *We now move south to travel back to Accrington on the line from Stubbins Junction, the route of trains from Manchester Victoria, via Clifton Junction and Bury, to Colne and Skipton. The extract from the L&YR Appendix to the Working Timetable (WTT) for 1884 shows the steeper gradients on the route. (Lancashire and Yorkshire Railway Society)*

STEEP INCLINES IN THE EAST LANCASHIRE DIVISION.

CLIFTON JUNCTION TO ACCRINGTON.

	Miles	Gradient
From Molyneux Junction to Ringley Road, rising for		1 in 96
" Ringley Road to Radcliffe, falling for	1	1 in 120
" 1½ miles beyond Radcliffe to Bury, rising for	1	1 in 132
" 1 mile beyond Bury to Stubbins Junction, rising for	3¼	1 in 132
" Stubbins Junction to ¾ mile beyond Haslingden, rising for	5	1 in 78
Thence to Baxenden, falling for	¾	1 in 100
" Baxenden to Accrington, falling for	2	1 in 40

➘ X. The Stubbins Junction to Accrington line was not the highest on the L&YR network, that honour belonging to Britannia on the Bacup to Rochdale line. However, from the moment it left the Bury to Bacup line at Stubbins Junction it was a five mile climb, at an average of 1:78, to the 771ft summit between Haslingden and Baxenden. Between Stubbins and Helmshore there were substantial viaducts at Lumb and then Ravenshore with a further one north of Helmshore. The descent to Accrington was even more severe, at 1:40 for two of the three miles. This map extract shows the Accrington line diverging just before Stubbins station, whose platforms were only on the Bacup line, the present day East Lancashire Railway to Rawtenstall.

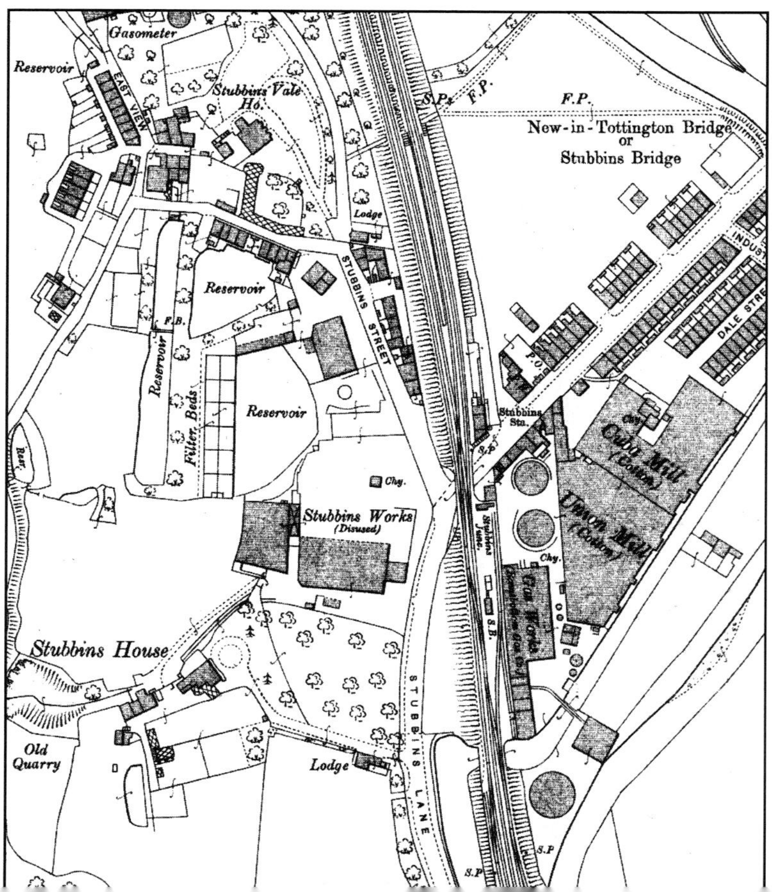

29. A Bury to Rawtenstall Cravens DMU calls at the surviving platform at Stubbins on 27th May 1972, one week before the singled line to Rawtenstall closed to passengers. The Accrington line tracks ran behind the in use platform and the rails can just be seen. Nearly six years after closure they were still in place because of an intended preservation scheme to Helmshore and Grane Road. The climb to the Baxenden summit began immediately from the junction while the route to Bacup followed the Irwell Valley floor. (W.A. Camwell)

HELMSHORE

XI. Helmshore station opened with the line in 1848. It was part way down a steep hill on the main road through the village, which crossed the line at a level crossing. There were several large cotton mills nearby, one of which was adjacent to the station goods yard.

Pocket timetable from 1966.

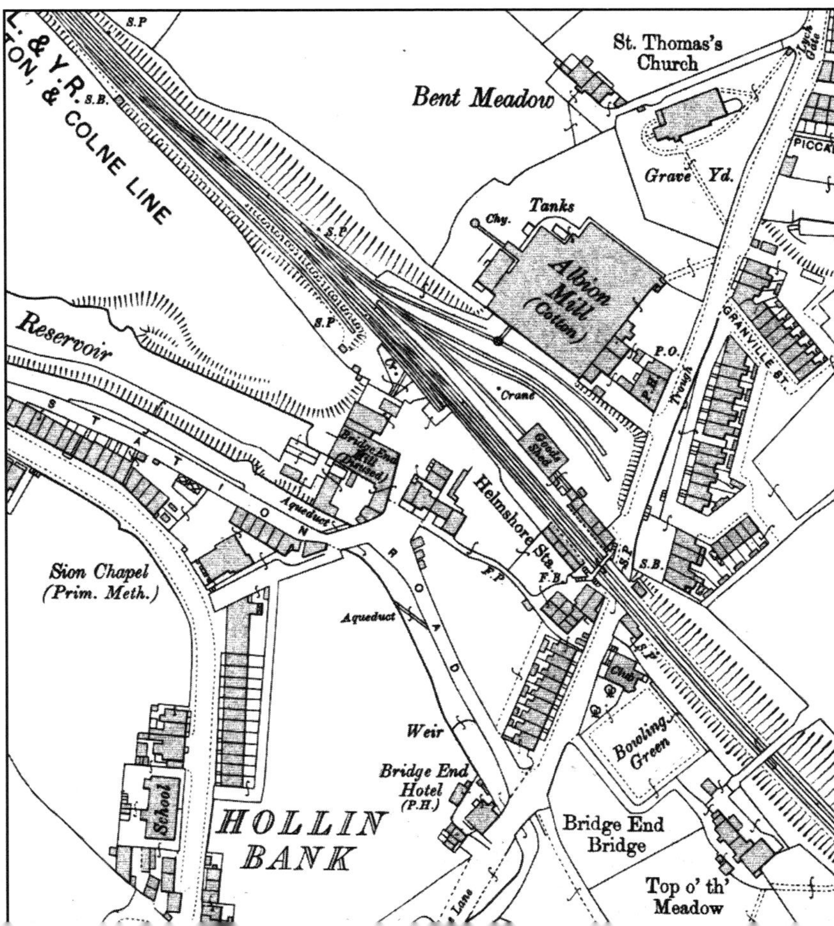

30. Helmshore station is two miles up the bank from Stubbins Junction. This view, looking towards Haslingden in L&YR days, is how it looked for most of its life. The large wooden goods shed can be seen behind the buildings on the up platform and handled much traffic from and for various cotton mills in the village but closed on 7th September 1964, two years before the line. The 1:78 climb continued through Haslingden to the summit near Baxenden. (Lens of Sutton Association)

31. Right up to closure Helmshore had a healthy passenger service. The 1964 timetable shows 15 weekday departures in each direction, the majority being Manchester Victoria to Colne or Skipton through trains, running via Clifton Junction and Bury, although a couple of these started from or terminated at Accrington or Bury. No Sunday service though. In later years the Cravens twin power car sets from Accrington shed were the mainstay of services. This DMU from Bury Bolton St was the last train to use the line, and therefore the last to call at Helmshore station, on Saturday 3rd December 1966. Photos of this train in Bury and Accrington are snow free but of course Helmshore is more elevated.
(The late David Dyson,
courtesy of Mike Taylor)

32. Soon after closure, with track still in place, Helmshore became an early base for the East Lancashire Railway Preservation Society (ELRPS). They rented the station and laid a siding for some industrial locos and goods wagons. The steep gradient down to Stubbins meant they were never allowed to keep their stock on the running lines. Over the 1970 Summer Bank Holiday a gala weekend was held and Black 5 (in Green) no. 44806 attended, by rail in light steam behind BR Type 2 no. D5283, which also delivered a rail mounted hand crane to the society. 44806 remained in steam both days, seen here on the Saturday. The proposed heritage line would have run from Stubbins through Helmshore to terminate at the site of Grane Road Goods. However, the preservationists encountered a number of difficulties and, when the former Castlecroft Goods Shed at Bury became available, the society moved there, from where it grew into the East Lancashire Railway we know today. Helmshore station was later demolished and housing now covers the site. (David A Ingham)

Grane Road Goods

XII. Mid-way between Helmshore and Haslingden stations was Grane Road Goods Siding. The opening date of this has not been ascertained but the stone quarries around Haslingden will have been a source of revenue for the railway from an early date, if not the opening of the line. A narrow gauge tramway from transhipment sidings wound around the nearby reservoirs to an inclined plane that brought stone down from the quarries on Musbury Heights. Just across the road from the goods yard was another inclined plane leading to Hutch Bank quarry. The yard also served nearby cotton mills and dye factories and a separate siding served the local gas works. Had the ELRPS reopened the line through Helmshore this would always have been the northern limit of operations, as from the closure of the line it was known that the trackbed through Haslingden station was required for the A56 bypass road.

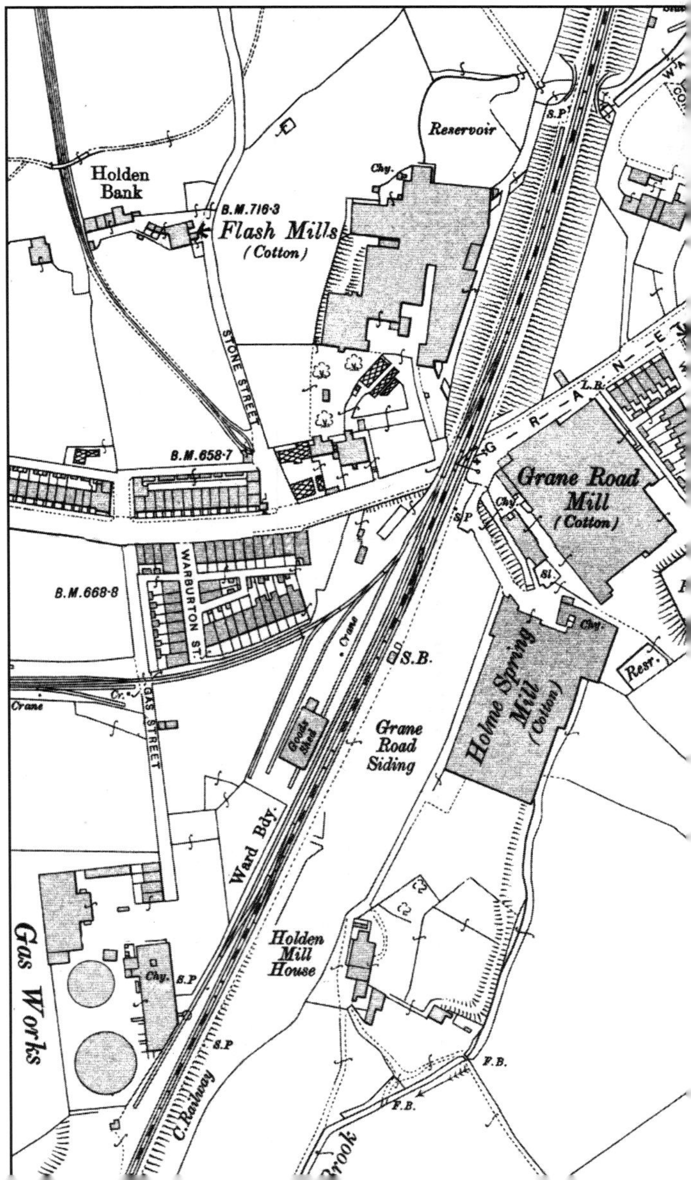

HASLINGDEN

Haslingden station opened with the line on 17th August 1848. It had a substantial goods shed and yard but was remote from the town centre, with its frequent bus services from Accrington. It closed to passengers on 7th November 1960, except for occasional excursions while the line remained open.

➔ 33. An early photo of Haslingden station, taken from North Hag, under which the line tunnelled immediately south of the station platforms. The extensive goods facilities can be seen and the substantial single storey building on the Manchester platform. Passengers alighting here had to negotiate the goods yard then climb a steep hill to the main road. From there it was a half mile walk into the town centre. Although goods traffic outlasted the passenger services it was gradually lost to road haulage and the yard closed on 2nd November 1964. (John Alsop collection)

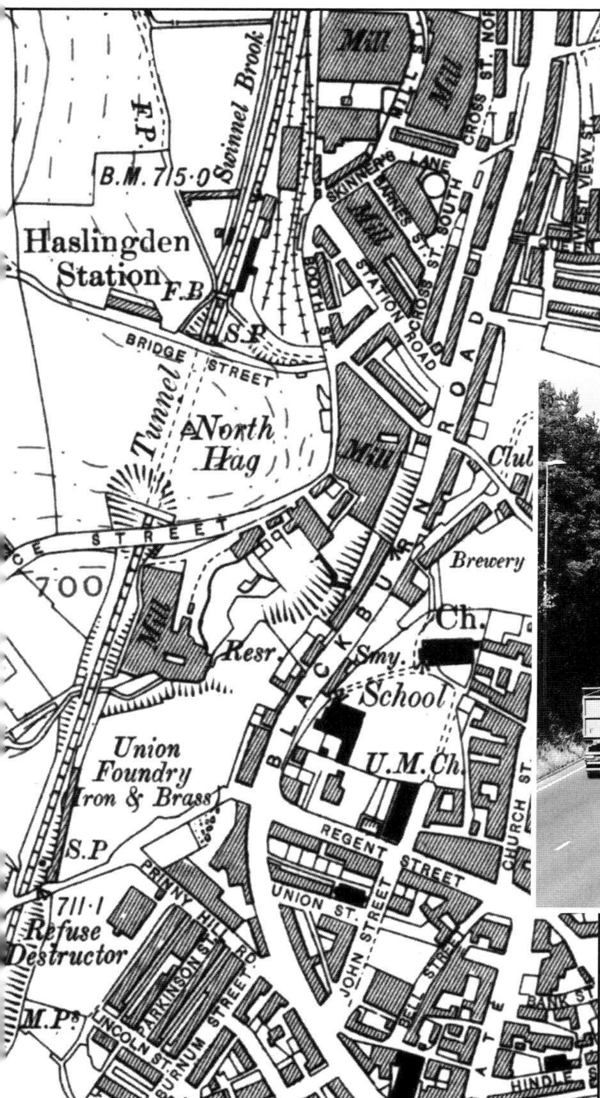

← XIII. When railways close it is common to see cuttings filled in and embankments removed but the complete removal of a railway tunnel and its associated hill is more unusual. This is a 1911 6ins to 1 mile map extract of Haslingden station and the North Hag tunnel.

Inset: The photograph shows the same location on 1st September 2022, viewed from the site of the south portal, looking north where the hill and tunnel once stood towards the site of Haslingden station. (Mark Bartlett)

BAXENDEN

XIV. Baxenden station opened with the line on 17th August 1848 but was some distance from Baxenden, closer to the smaller village of Rising Bridge. With frequent buses on the main road, and only two miles from Accrington, the station closed to passengers on 10th September 1951, although goods traffic lasted until 6th February 1961. Since closure Baxenden Chemicals, shown on this map, has expanded over much of the trackbed and uses part of it as an access road. On the north side of the line Hollands Pies have also expanded their factory (shown as Cotton Mill) and obliterated most of the station remains.

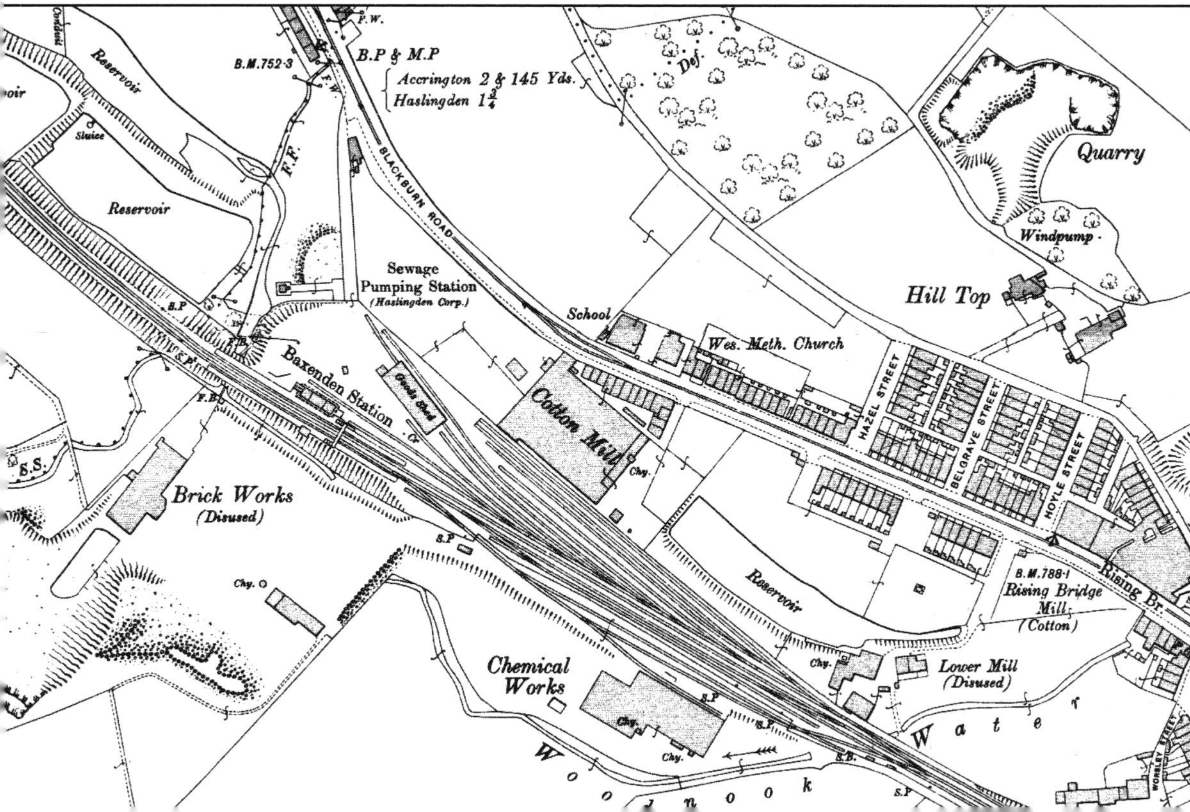

34. Baxenden station, in 1950, looking towards Haslingden. The single storey building is similar to those at Haslingden and Helmshore. The platforms are deserted and the station would close to passengers the following year. Traffic in the goods yard, under the shadow of the Hollands Pies' chimney, looks healthier and would last a further 10 years. The signal box controlling the yard access can be seen in the distance. Trains ran through Baxenden's platforms for a further 15 years after the last passenger train called. Part of the Bury platform is still in situ at the end of the public greenway from Accrington. (Lancashire and Yorkshire Railway Society)

35. Baxenden Station signal box was sited some way south of the station platforms, by the goods yard access points. It was a tall structure, squeezed onto railway land, with the brickwork section quite narrow but the cabin itself slightly cantilevered over the down line. As traffic declined, Shoe Mill signal box on Baxenden Bank closed and Baxenden was then the first box after Accrington South. This picture dates from the late 1960s, after the line had closed completely but before the tracks were lifted. The vandals have begun to attack the box windows and it would get worse before the demolition gang arrived. (Lancashire and Yorkshire Railway Society)

Baxenden Bank

WORKING OF ACCRINGTON INCLINE.

Drivers and Guards of Passenger Trains must have their Trains well under command before passing the top of the Incline. All Goods Trains must be brought to a stand at the top of the Incline, and the Guards must pin down sufficient Brakes to allow the Train to descend in safety. The speed of Trains on approaching Accrington Station must not exceed 4 miles an hour.

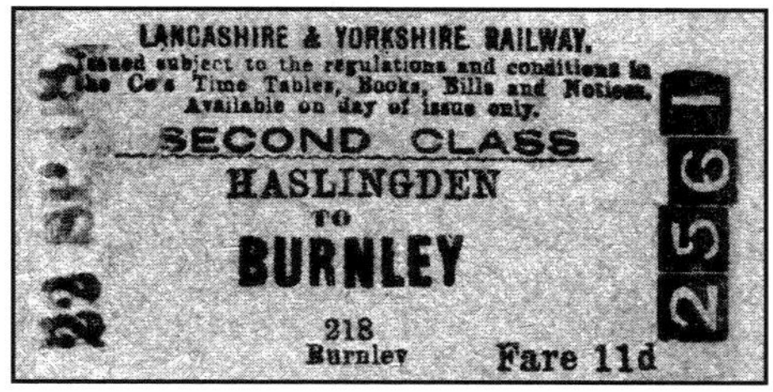

This notorious incline climbed at mainly 1:40 for southbound services, straight from the platform at Accrington. Travelling northwards it was an equally steep descent with the associated difficulties for unbraked goods trains. The above extract from the Appendix to the 1884 WTT shows the instructions for descending to Accrington. It is incredible to think that despite these difficulties the L&YR slipped coaches for Accrington at the foot of this bank. (Lancashire and Yorkshire Railway Society)

36. 'Crab' 2-6-0 no. 42716 from Rose Grove shed approaches Shoe Mill signal box climbing the 1:40 gradient on what is believed to be the evening freight service from Burnley to Moston. Despite the gradient the crew look relaxed as they pose for the camera but the fireman will soon be back on the shovel. Ahead, the signal box can be seen to be closed, dating this photo between 1962 and 1965 when the Crab was withdrawn. The signal in the foreground has no glass in the off position so has perhaps become a fixed distant for Accrington South Junction. This location is now a public greenway, but heavily wooded rather than the open scene here. Shoe Mill box and the adjacent viaduct are now demolished but a replacement footbridge allows the old railway to be followed from Accrington to Baxenden. (The late David Dyson, courtesy of Mike Taylor)

37. Directly at the foot of Baxenden Bank, Accrington South Junction was where the chord to West Junction diverged from the main line (see map IX, opposite picture 22). Black 5 no. 45388 looks ready to tackle the climb but a closer look tells a different story. The lifted track section, sleeper on the up line and armless signals show this is 1967, with the line closed but not yet lifted. The train is a parcels from Colne to Preston that has stopped at the parcels office and will reverse out to continue. Later, a single siding, with buffers replacing the semaphore, would suffice for the few years until the traffic ceased altogether. The buffers on the left are the headshunt for Eagle St. coal depot, which had closed in October 1964. To the right of those are the steel parapets of the low viaduct over the mill reservoir. Also of interest is the short sand drag with exit points on the down line. (The late David Dyson, courtesy of Mike Taylor)

38. These columns carried the line to Stubbins over a mill reservoir immediately south of Accrington station. The bridge decking was removed but the columns left in place and when the water was part drained they became part of an urban park. They were painted bright red when the park first opened but that has faded to more of a dusky pink. They mark the route of the line and the path leads on to the old trackbed greenway up the bank to Baxenden. (Mark Bartlett)

3. Accrington North Junction to Padiham Junction

Accrington North Junction and the Viaduct

➔ *The lines from Blackburn and Stubbins Junction converge at Accrington North Junction to continue towards Burnley and Colne. A gradient profile for this section is shown on the right.*

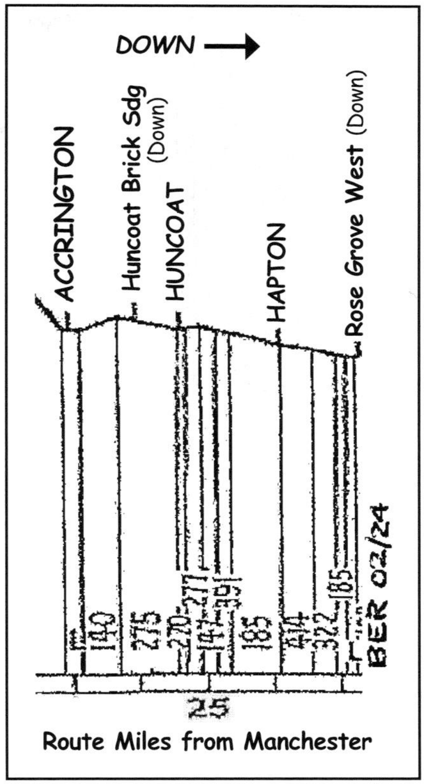

39. Accrington had signal boxes at the West, South and North junctions. South closed with the line to Stubbins in 1966 but West lasted a little longer. Accrington North was a secondhand L&YR structure, moved here in 1939 after use elsewhere, and was the last to close, in late 1973. On 13th April 1969, A3 4-6-2 no. 4472 *Flying Scotsman*, at that time running with two tenders and the only steam locomotive allowed on BR, rounded the sharp curve off the viaduct and passed North box. Over 50 years later this loco is still pulling the crowds across the country. The single line stub, serving just the parcels office, is in the foreground but would close within a couple of years. (Tom Bartlett)

40. The 19-arch Accrington Viaduct curves over the town with a 10mph speed restriction at the station end. The impressive structure is Grade II listed. On 1st March 1986, a BRCW class 104 DMU arrives on a stopping service from Colne. For many years the 'Birms' operated as three-car sets on services such as Manchester to Blackpool North but as power car twins eked out their final years of service on local stopping trains. Huncoat Power Station can be seen top right. (Paul D. Shannon)

Huncoat Brick Sidings

XV. Huncoat Brick Sidings signal box was on the northwest side of the line opposite Accrington cemetery; the sidings ran from here to Huncoat station. A mineral line ran north-westwards branching into two separate lines, one to Whinney Hill Brickworks and the other to Accrington Brick and Tile Works. The first of these mineral lines around Huncoat opened around 1900 and the system expanded between the wars servicing collieries, brick works and chemical works. Huncoat Colliery had over 100 coke ovens and a fleet of saddle tanks operated over the network of lines conveying coal, coke and bricks between plants and to the exchange sidings. This 2½ ins to 1 mile map from 1937 shows the area at its height. It was particularly busy during the 1950s but there was then a rapid decline and by 1970 these connected branch lines had all closed.

The standard gauge locos that operated this surface network, sporting names such as *Lark*, *Linnet*, *Kestrel* and *Raven*, have all been scrapped but a 2ft gauge Hunslet mine loco, that worked underground at Huncoat, was bought by the Talyllyn railway and now operates their works trains sporting the name *Alf*.

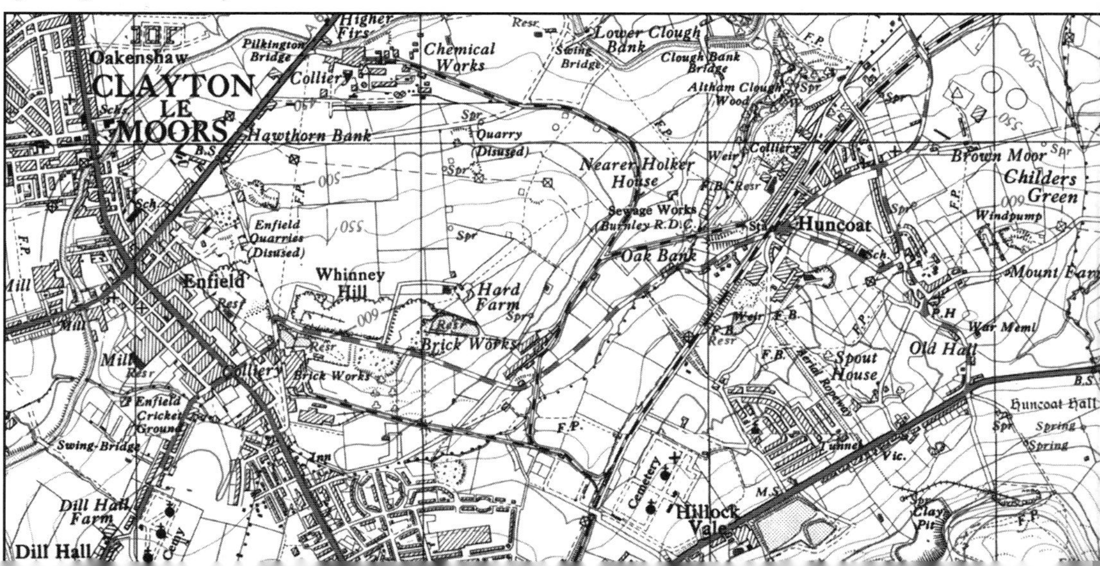

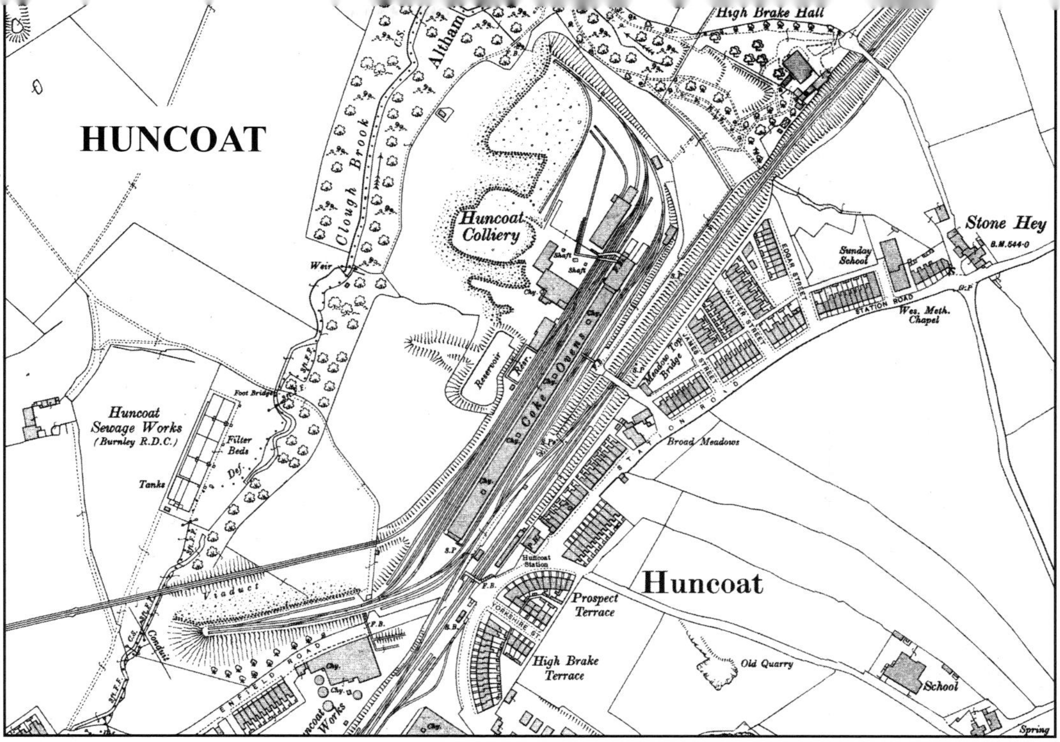

XVI. The first station at Huncoat was opened on 1st December 1848, on Altham Lane where the power station was later constructed. The second was opened on the present site in the village by 1881. A local petition complained about 'the disgraceful accommodation'. The 1890 OS map shows the signal box on the down side of line and staggered platforms either side of level crossing. In 1902, to accommodate an expansion of goods facilities, the up platform moved to its present site opposite the down and a new signal box built on the up side. The larger goods yard dealt with mill traffic, coal and bricks. This 1911 map shows the station and adjacent colliery with its huge array of coke ovens.

41. A new station at Huncoat was built in 1912 from distinctive local brick. It had full facilities including a booking office, general waiting room, ladies room, parcel office, porter's room, lamp room and toilets all being provided. This view looks south, probably in early BR days before the maroon LMR enamel totems and other signs were fitted. (John Alsop collection)

42. With main line steam only days away from the end, Stanier 8F 2-8-0 no. 48476 is on a west bound freight passing through Huncoat on 24th July 1968. On the left is Huncoat Colliery, along with a link to the down line. After a very busy period in the 1950s the pit had closed on 9th February that year but rakes of wooden bodied coal wagons are still in the yard. These had been used on the local works system and the short industrial line to Huncoat Power Station, whose chimneys can be seen top right. 48476 was to haul one of the 4th August End of Steam specials just over a week later but was then withdrawn and scrapped. (A. Hutton courtesy ColourRail.co.uk)

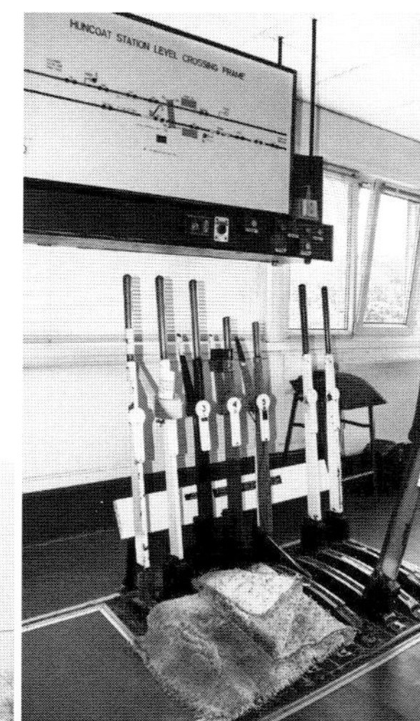

43. Class 37 no. 37519 passes Huncoat with 6Z51, the 11.30 Blackburn to Lackenby on 31st March 1989. A variety of wagons were used to carry hot-rolled coil steel to Gilbraith's Blackburn depot. Huncoat signal box had opened in 1902 as local brickworks expanded and traffic increased. It had, unusually, two gate wheels as there was another level crossing adjacent to the main line one which allowed colliery traffic to cross the road. All the sidings had gone by 1970 and from 1973 it was downgraded to a gate box working under the supervision of Preston Power Box. The original 40 lever frame was replaced with one of just eight levers (inset), of which only four were in use. It closed in 2014 and was demolished the year after. (Paul D. Shannon and David A. Ingham)

Huncoat Power Station

Huncoat Power Station was rail served both from the main line and a mineral line from Huncoat Colliery. Construction started in 1949 and the first generator set was operational in June 1952. The station gradually expanded until the fifth and final set was commissioned in September 1957. A wharf was constructed for canal barges but the colliery output meant this was never needed. Power generation ceased in 1984 and demolition took place over several years.

44. During July 1968, the last full month of BR steam working, Stanier 8F 2-8-0 48393 is amongst the 16T mineral wagons in the sidings at Huncoat Power Station, no doubt after delivering a load of coal and waiting for a rake of empties to return to the supplying colliery. Nearby Huncoat Colliery, which supplied the power station by a half mile long mineral railway, had closed a few months earlier and for the rest of its life the station received coal supplies by rail from collieries further afield. (Peter Fidczuk collection)

45. Fireless 0-6-0F *Huncoat No.3* (Hawthorn 3746/1929) was built for the Oldham Electricity Works but later moved to Huncoat. Here it propels 16 tonners into the Huncoat tippler in May 1975, a task it must have performed innumerable times. Conveyor belts took the coal across the main line to the plant. The tyres on the loco look very worn but it continued in service until the station ceased generating in 1984. *No.3* then moved into preservation at the Tanfield Railway. (Mark Bartlett)

HAPTON

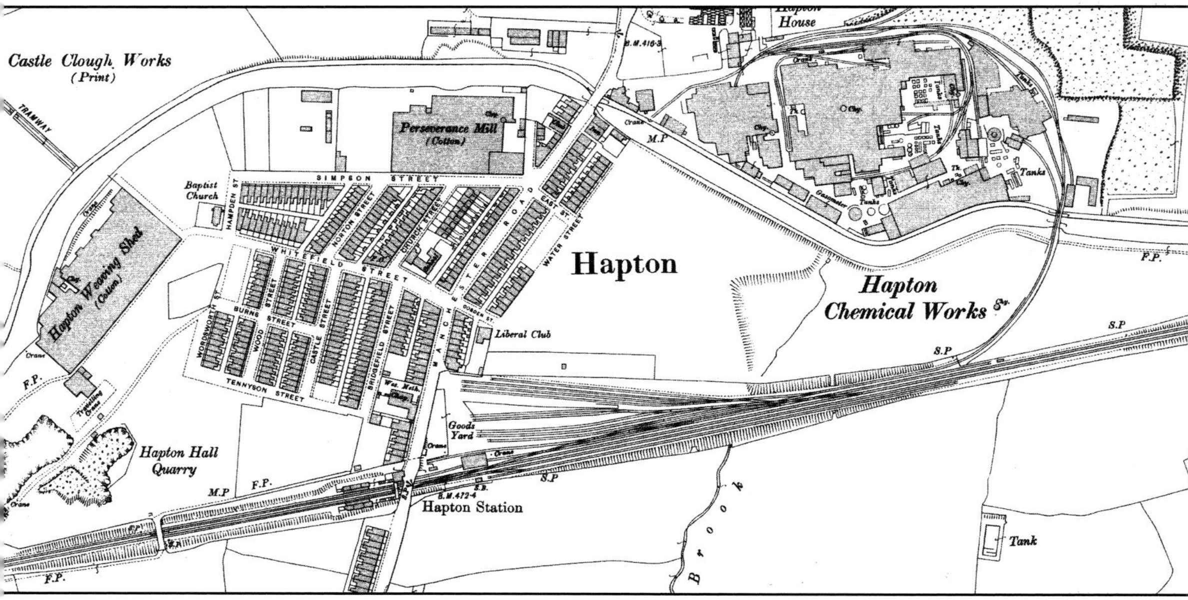

XVII. Hapton opened around 1st May 1862. A modern map would show the 1983 M65 motorway running alongside the railway. To the east of the station the goods yard closed on 25th January 1965 and the motorway has obliterated this and the private siding that crossed the canal to access William Blythe's Hapton Chemical Works. In fact, just beyond here, the canal has also had to be diverted slightly to clear a path for the M65. To the west a long footbridge now spans the line and motorway providing a good vantage point. Blythe's have also relocated with their site turned over to housing.

46. It is 24th July 1968 and normal BR steam working is almost finished as 45156 *Ayrshire Yeomanry* takes a short freight towards Accrington passing through Hapton. As one of the few named Black 5s this was something of a celebrity and hauled one of the Farewell to Steam 4th August specials, following which it was withdrawn and sadly scrapped. (A. Hutton courtesy ColourRail.com)

47. Hapton, now a request stop, is the least used station between Blackburn and Colne, recording 15,110 passengers in 2019-20. The buildings have gone, as has the footbridge, but the platforms can be accessed by ramps from the road. The platforms have been cut back too but the old stanchions at the Accrington end can be seen. 156412 runs slowly through the station on 22nd August 2023 heading for Colne, but no hands are signalling the driver and it continues on its way. This view from a footbridge to the west of the station shows the close proximity of the M65. (Mark Bartlett)

Padiham Junction

NORTH LANCASHIRE LOOP LINE.

All Through Trains which consist, on arrival at Rose Grove, of more Wagons than the Engine can haul over the Incline on the Loop without assistance, will run via Accrington.

48. Stanier 8F 2-8-0 no. 48340 is passing Padiham Junction, controlled by Rose Grove West signal box, with a long train of 16T mineral empties in 1968. The Padiham Loop line, by then just a one mile freight branch to Padiham power station, curves away behind the train, which is returning from another Lancashire power station. For 1968 the locomotive is commendably clean and it remained in service right up to 3rd August but was scrapped after withdrawal. (Lens of Sutton Association)

4. The Padiham Loop

We return to Great Harwood Junction, near Blackburn, to journey eastwards over the Padiham Loop to Rose Grove before continuing to Skipton. Bearing left at the junction the line drops down at 1:90 towards Great Harwood, three and a half miles away and the first station on the line.

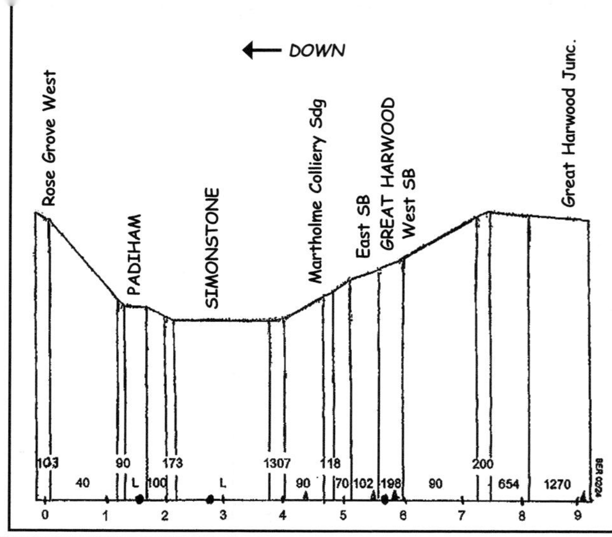

49. Stanier 5MT 4-6-0 no. 45275, with the regulator open, approaches the site of Great Harwood Junction heading east around 1967. Behind the loco are two DMUs, one a Derby (later class 108) set and the other a Cravens (later class 105) so presumably one of these had failed and the Black 5 had come to the rescue. In between the up line and up loop is an L&YR 'parachute' water tank but it looks rusty and is marked with a white cross indicating it has been condemned. 45275 sports a 10F Rose Grove shed plate. It had transferred there from Holyhead in August 1966 and remained until withdrawn in October 1967, after which it was scrapped at Cashmores, Great Bridge during February 1968. (Lancashire and Yorkshire Railway Society)

Extract from the L&YR Appendix to the WTT for 1884, showing the opening times for the signal boxes controlling the Padiham Loop. (Lancashire and Yorkshire Railway Society)

Padiham Branch

Absolute Block.	...	...	Padiham Junction			Continuously	
	3	580	" Station, East		280	"	●
	...	300	" " West			6-0 a.m. Mondays to 6 0 a.m. Sundays	●
	1	...	Simonstone			6-0 a.m. Mondays to 9-30 p.m. Sundays	●
	2	860	Great Harwood	175	470	6-0 a.m. Mondays to 9-30 p.m. Sundays	●
	1	1160	" " Intermediate			7-0 a.m. to 7-0 p.m. Week Days	
	1	1320	" " Junction			Continuously	●

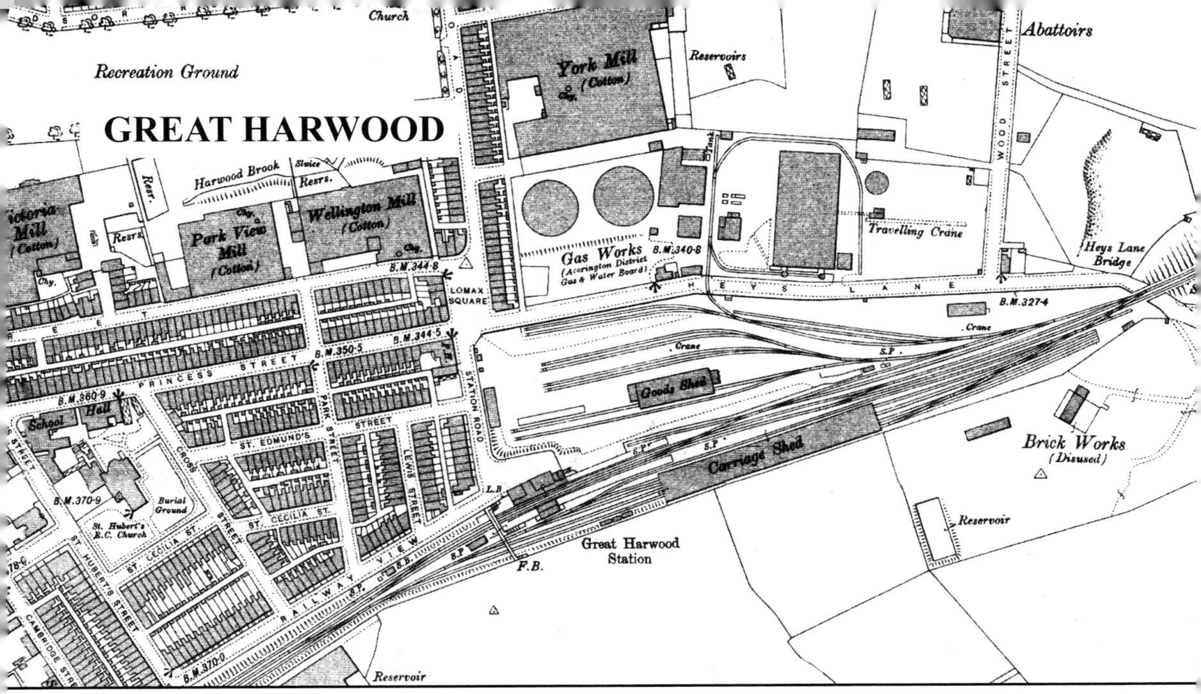

XVIII. Great Harwood station opened to passengers on 15th October 1877 and had the usual range of passenger facilities and a goods yard but there was also a four road carriage shed alongside the up platform. The carriage sidings were in use until the 1960s, although in later years the shed was roofless. The West signal box controlled the west end access to the carriage sidings. The East box controlled the east end access and also that to the goods yard.

50. Was the photographer who captured this Whitsuntide procession in Great Harwood around 1910 also a railway enthusiast? West signal box is just behind the wall and the station itself is on the curving lines with the platforms visible beyond the bridge. To the right is the four road carriage shed. The procession is on the terraced street known as Railway View. The houses are still there, but now overlook a public greenspace on the trackbed. Station Road joins this road at right angles, where the main station entrance was situated but today, everything to the east of the footbridge has been covered with business units. (John Alsop collection)

51. Looking westwards at Great Harwood around 1952, five years before regular passenger services ceased. After that date, for a further seven years, freight trains and through excursions for the Lancashire coastal resorts continued to pass through. During Great Harwood's holiday fortnight the station would open and summer excursion trains would call but all this ceased after the summer of 1964 and the line, and Great Harwood goods yard, closed on 2nd November. The terraced houses on Railway View are all that can still be seen today, renamed as Hameldon View after a nearby hill. (John Alsop collection).

Martholme Viaduct

XIX. The Padiham Loop was said to be, mile for mile, the most expensive line built by the Lancashire and Yorkshire Railway. The curving 10-arch viaduct at Martholme takes the line across the River Calder and will have been a large factor in those costs, as were the lengthy and sometimes unstable embankments to the east of Great Harwood. Approaching the viaduct, the line curved to run due north and passed sidings for a short branch to Martholme Pit. This colliery was worked out by 1921 and closed, along with the sidings and signal box that controlled them. As the line entered the viaduct it began a long sweeping curve, at the end of which it was heading south east towards Simonstone.

↘ 52. The east elevation of Martholme Viaduct in September 2008. The bridge trackbed, 75ft above the River Calder, was not accessible at this time although the line could be walked from the outskirts of Great Harwood to the south end of the bridge. Since then the deck has been reopened as part of the Martholme Greenway, but it is not yet a through route as the north end is still fenced off. It does however provide an elevated view of the surrounding Lancashire scenery, and the embankment of the old railway curving towards Simonstone. (Mark Bartlett)

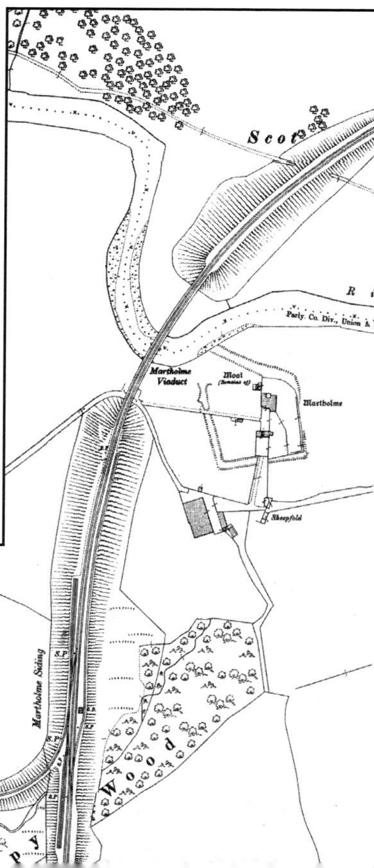

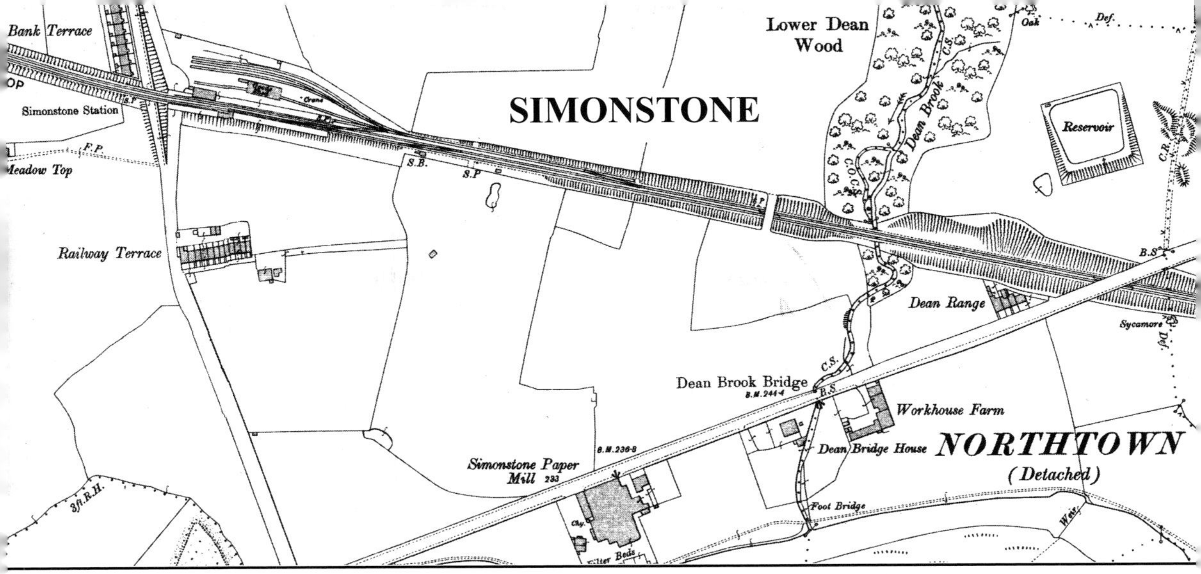

XX. Simonstone was the smallest of the three loop line stations, some distance downhill from the village of Read that it served. It had a small goods yard on the north side. The map shows the line around 1913 but the triangle of land to the south of the railway was later used as the site of Mullards electrical factory. This was due to open in 1956, when rumours were starting to circulate that the line might close. Managers at the factory requested that the 6.32am service from Blackburn be retimed 10 minutes earlier so that up to 400 workers might use the train for work. Not only was this refused but, the day the new factory opened, the Simonstone stop of that train was taken out of the timetable. All other trains continued to call until scheduled services ceased the following year.

53. Simonstone in L&YR days, looking towards Martholme. The station appears well-kept but just two people are in view. To the right of the fence some sheeted wagons can be seen in the goods yard. In October 1957 this became a coal depot, no longer handling general traffic. The following month the station closed to passengers and, unlike Padiham and Great Harwood, did not handle summer excursions. The coal depot closed with the line in November 1964. (John Alsop collection)

54. On 30th May 1968, this was the scene on Simonstone Lane as the girder bridge immediately east of the station was dismantled. The stone abutments were left in place and a dip in the roadway passing between them is today an easily visible reminder of the station's existence. However, nearby but hidden, in 2023 the goods shed was the only railway building to survive on the whole of the Loop Line. (Burnley Civic Trust Heritage Image Collection - bcthic.org)

Padiham Power Station

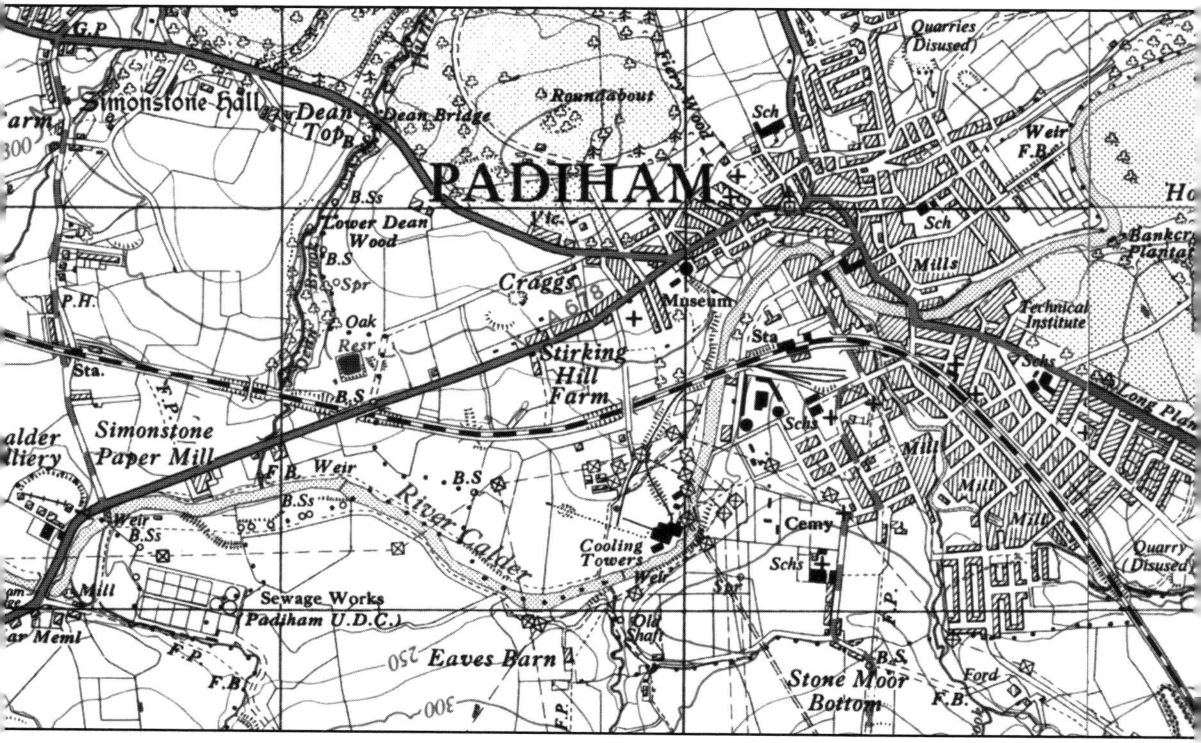

XXI. Padiham A power station, just west of the station and alongside the River Calder, first generated electricity in 1927. Padiham B was authorised for construction in 1957 and commissioned in 1962. With the closure of most of the loop line in November 1964, the power stations became the limit of operations, shortened to just over one mile of track from Rose Grove. Padiham A closed in 1969 but Padiham B continued to generate until 1993. This 2½ ins to 1 mile map dated 1947 shows the power station site, station and goods yard and the start of the climb to Rose Grove.

55. Looking like yet another pile up of Reverend Awdry's Troublesome Trucks, BR Type 2 7654 sits on the old loop line ballast, opposite the power station, on 23rd July 1971. The loaded coal train had run away coming down the bank from Rose Grove and this was the result. No fatalities thankfully but the driver and secondman were injured jumping out of the cab when it became clear the train was out of control. In those pre-RAIB days a BR spokesman said, 'There will be an enquiry but the results won't be made public'. No. 7654 was repaired after the incident, becoming 25304, and remained in service until 1982. (Burnley Civic Trust Heritage Image Collection - bcthic.org)

56. AB474/1961, 0-4-0DM *No.2*, stored in front of Padiham B Power Station on 2nd September 1988. With sister AB 473/1961, *No.1*, it shunted the 16 tonners into the tipplers from new. Much coal came from Lancashire and Yorkshire pits but also from Nottingham, Durham, Cumbria and Fife as well as imports. In 1974, Unit 1 at Padiham B was converted to oil firing and tanker trains began running down the branch to an unloading facility but did not need the shunters. The sheeted steeple cab electric *No.2* was one of four used at Kearsley PS. After Kearsley closed in 1982, two of these went to Heysham Power Station and were converted to battery operation. *No.2* was used to provide spare parts but was then preserved in its own right. (Gordon Edgar)

57. Although Unit 1 at Padiham B was converted to oil firing, Unit 2 remained a coal plant and received its first coal train for a decade on 16th November 1991, when BR hired open box wagons from NACCO to deliver coal from Maryport for National Power. BR class 60 no. 60032 *William Booth* looks brand new as an excavator unloads coal from a 35 wagon train. The coal is piled over redundant tracks in front of the old tippler building. One vehicle from another rake of loaded wagons can just be seen alongside the redundant oil unloading facility that had kept the branch active in the 1980s. (Paul D. Shannon)

PADIHAM

58. An L&YR Barton-Wright 0-6-2T calls at Padiham with a service for Great Harwood and Blackburn. The station opened with the line in 1877, sited on a curve at the foot of the 1:40 bank from Rose Grove. On the south side was a goods yard with a shed and several sidings. These engines were introduced the same year the Padiham Loop opened and were the first 0-6-2Ts in the UK. Most had 4ft 6in wheels for freight work but some had 5ft 1in diameter for passenger working. They were built in batches up to 1883. Most were withdrawn before WWI but some lasted into LMS days. (Lancashire and Yorkshire Railway Society)

NORTH LANCASHIRE LOOP LINE.

From Padiham Junction to Padiham Station, falling for	1¼	1 in 40
" ¼ mile beyond Padiham Station, falling for	½	1 in 100
Thence rising for	3¼	1 in 90

59. Enthusiasts from the 'Rossendale Forester Rail Tour' swarm over the closed platforms at Padiham on 3rd December 1966. This had run over the Clifton Junction to Bacup line and then from Ramsbottom to Accrington as these lines (except for Bury to Rawtenstall) were closing that weekend. Stanier 4MT 2-6-4T no. 42644 had brought the five coaches down from Rose Grove and was running round. It was joined by Ivatt 2MT 2-6-0 no. 46437 to go back up the bank and then over Copy Pit to return to Manchester. (Burnley Civic Trust Heritage Image Collection - bcthic.org).

60. This is the start of the 1:40 bank from Padiham to Rose Grove, immediately to the east of Padiham station. After the last power station train ran in 1993 the rails stayed in place for a further 15 years. In 2010 the trackbed was finally converted into a greenway with a tarmac surface. In days of steam the banking of trains up this fearsome gradient between the houses was a well-known spectacle for the residents of the town, vividly described in Stuart Taylor's series of books, *Journeys by Excursion Train from East Lancashire*. (Mark Bartlett)

61. As we have seen, building a power station near the foot of a 1:40 gradient tests locomotive and train braking power rather than horsepower. For years, unfitted coal trains would drop down the bank with brakes pinned down. Going back up the empty trains still required banking in steam days. Later trains for Padiham, oil and coal, had continuous brakes which made the descent easier. Following the national miners' strike there was a policy of maintaining a minimum of three months, and ideally six months, stocks at power stations. When Padiham B was earmarked to close in 1993, trains moved the stockpile to Rugeley Power Station. That meant taking loaded trains up the bank and, even with powerful class 60 diesels, the wagons were split for the climb and recoupled at Rose Grove. 60047 *Robert Owen* is seen part way up the gradient with the first half of what is believed to be the last train on the branch, on 23rd July 1993. Padiham B ceased generating a few weeks later. (Mick Page)

5. Rose Grove to Earby

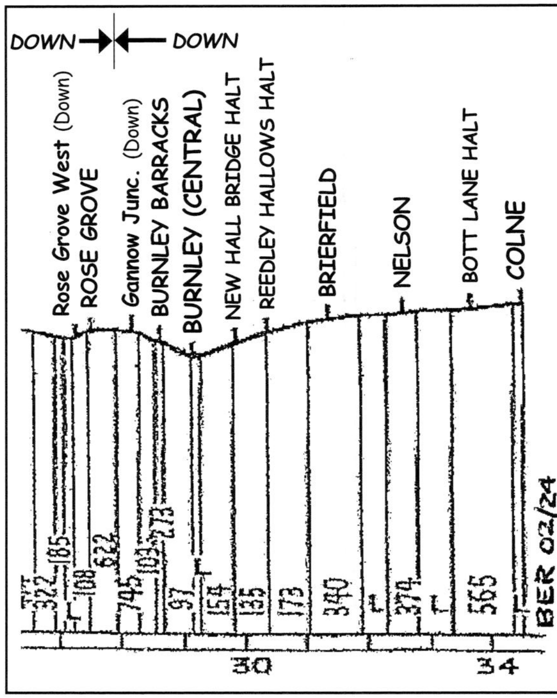

➔ *Gradient profile covering this section as far as Colne.*

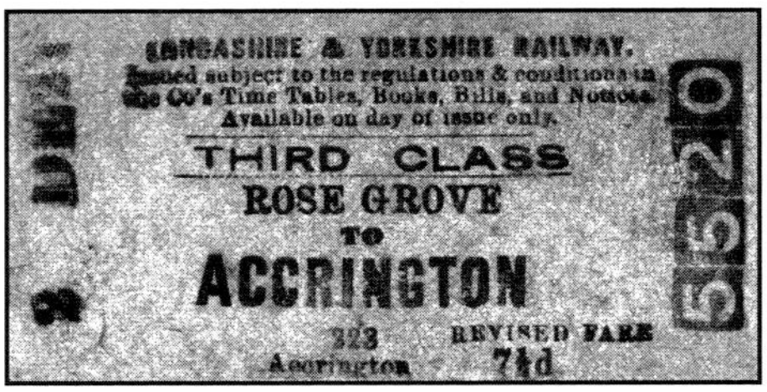

Rose Grove Shed

XXII. Rose Grove was a six road brick built L&YR shed opened in 1899. It was later rebuilt by the LMS and, after a fairly unsung life, achieved lasting fame as one of the last three steam sheds on BR.

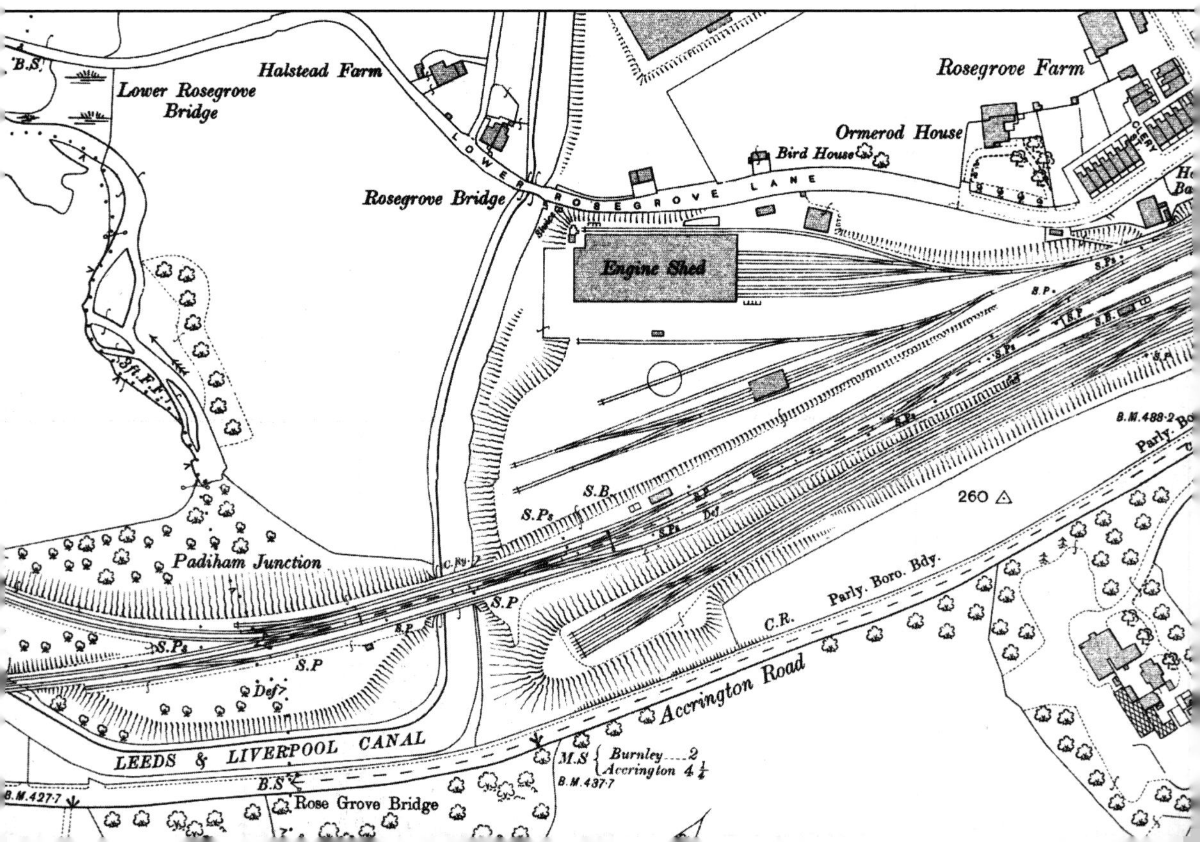

62. Rose Grove shed is seen on 15th April 1965. There was a hipped roof in LMS days that went in a rebuild. In BR days it was coded 24B, in the Accrington group of depots until 1961 when it became 10F under Carnforth. A Stanier Black 5 4-6-0 can be seen on the left and a Fowler 'Jinty' 3F 0-6-0T shunter on the right but the view is dominated by WD 2-8-0s, which had replaced the L&YR and later LMS 7F 0-8-0s. These WDs are a reminder that although LMS 8F 2-8-0s feature heavily in the numerous 'Last Days of Steam' photos around Rose Grove they were comparative latecomers, only ousting the WDs for a couple of years before steam finished altogether.
(T. Owen courtesy of ColourRail.co.uk)

63. Dereliction at Rose Grove Shed in 1974, just six years after it closed. A Cravens class 105 DMU heading for Colne slows to call at the station. The freight sidings still handle some traffic, mainly for the Lancashire power stations such as Huncoat, visible in the distance, and Padiham. The coaling plant has already gone and the six-road steam shed will soon be demolished to make way for the M65 motorway, which now passes the station running alongside the railway. (Mike Taylor)

ROSE GROVE

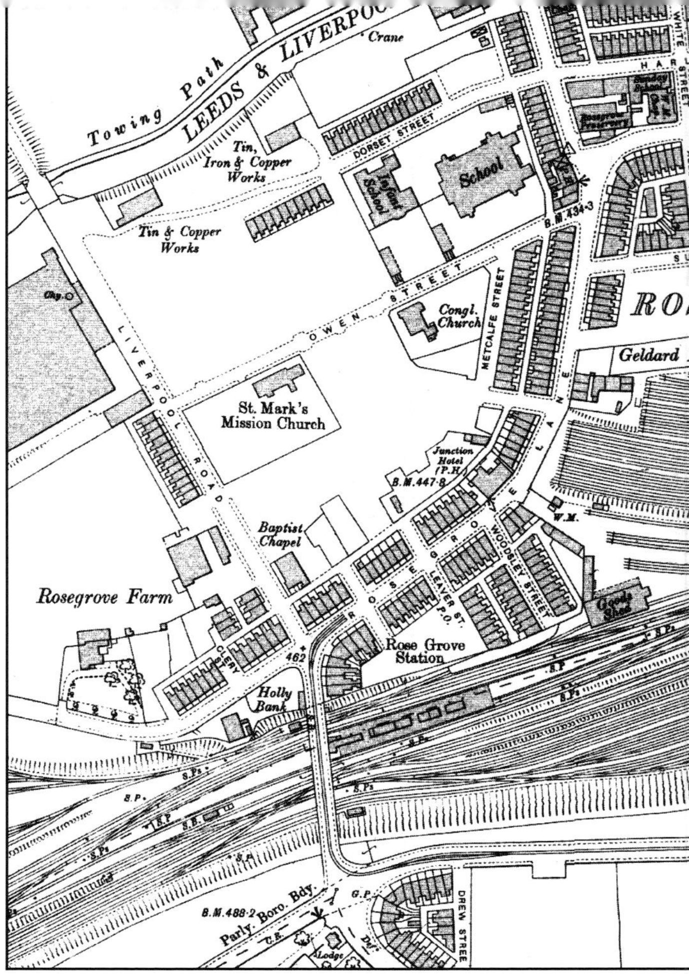

XXIII. Rose Grove station opened on 1st December 1848. The first station had two platforms but was later rebuilt as an island as shown on this 1913 25ins to 1 mile map extract. The substantial marshalling yards and humps are on both sides of the line. These yards were very busy right up to the 1960s but closed around 1970 as most of the freight traffic dried up leaving just a few block trains to serve the Lancashire power stations.

↓ 64. This early photograph shows the original layout at Rose Grove, with the down platform alongside the Goods Shed. Later, the L&YR rebuilt the station in their usual island platform style with a street level entrance on the overbridge and covered steps leading down to the platform buildings. This old station was demolished with further lines and sidings for freight trains laid in its place.
(John Alsop collection)

→ 65. A Cravens class 105 DMU arrives at Rose Grove on a Colne to Preston service on 20th July 1976. The station still has its platform buildings but they have lost their L&YR canopy. Freight continues to pass through the station but, beyond the long rake of mineral wagons, the down side marshalling yard beyond the goods shed has been lifted. However, class 40 no. 40137 is approaching the station with oil tanks destined for Padiham Power Station.
(Tom Heavyside)

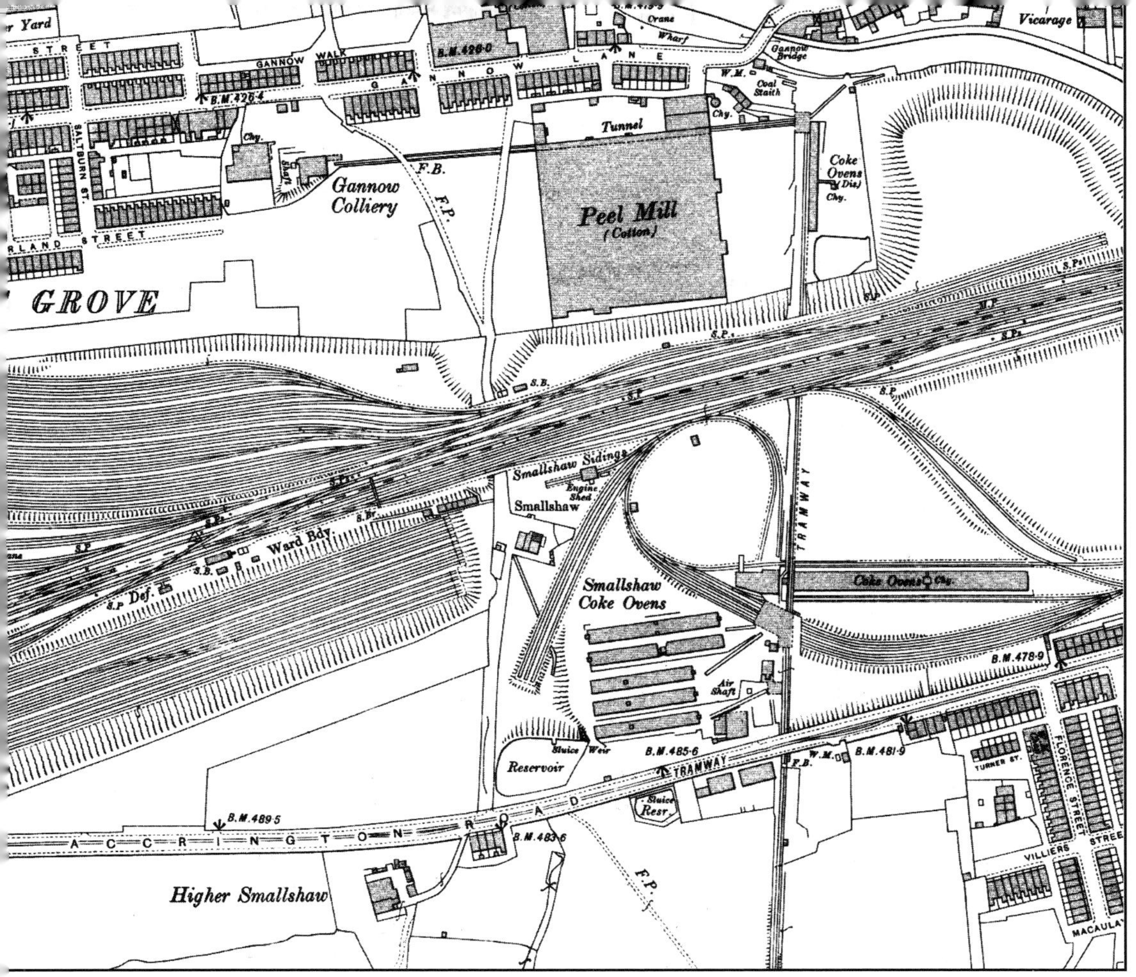

Yard
Vicarage
Crane
Wharf
Gannow Bridge
B.M. 426·0
GANNOW WALK
GANNOW LANE
STREET
B.M. 426·4
SALTBURN ST.
W.M.
Coal Staith
Chy.
Tunnel
Shaft
Gannow Colliery
F.B.
F.P.
Peel Mill
(Cotton)
Coke Ovens
(Dis)
RLAND STREET
GROVE
S.P.
S.B.
Smallshaw Sidings
Engine Shed
Smallshaw
TRAMWAY
Ward Bdy.
Def.
Smallshaw Coke Ovens
Coke Ovens
Air Shaft
B.M. 478·9
Sluice
Weir
Reservoir
B.M. 485·6
W.M.
B.M. 481·9
TURNER ST.
FLORENCE STREET
Resr.
B.M. 489·5
ACCRINGTON ROAD
B.M. 483·6
VILLIERS STREET
Higher Smallshaw
MACAULAY

66. Looking east towards Gannow Junction, from the entrance to Rose Grove on 7th March 2022, as two class 195/0 DMUs pass on a Blackpool North to York service. Although the station is tidy it has few facilities. To the right the up yard site now contains industrial units. To the left, bare trees allow a glimpse of the M65 Motorway. Apart from the two main running lines only one other track remains, namely the down goods loop, but there would be some severe damage to paintwork should a train attempt to use it. (John McIntyre)

Gannow Junction to Burnley Barracks

XXIV. With the Copy Pit line from Todmorden opening by the L&YR in 1849, just one year after the ELR reached Burnley, Gannow Junction has been a significant location on this line since the earliest days. It sits alongside but above the Leeds and Liverpool Canal at the point where it enters Gannow Tunnel. The signal box was originally on the north side of the line but later relocated by BR into the 'V' of the junction. It closed with the commissioning of Preston Power Box in 1973. From the turnout the line drops down to Burnley on a gradient of 1:103 with Barracks station situated at the end of the cutting, just before the canal bridge. The two intermediate bridges still span the cutting but are no longer used as the M65 runs alongside the line where the houses once stood.

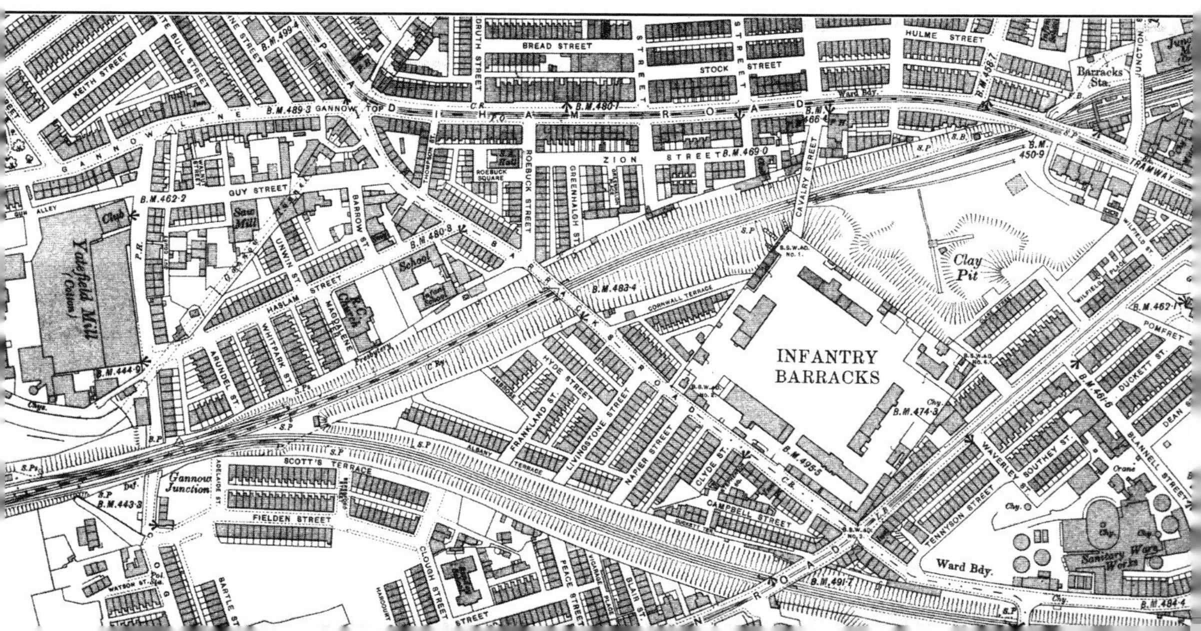

67. Taken from the position of the second Gannow Junction signal box, this view looks towards Rose Grove, with the tracks from the Copy Pit line curving in from the left, on 1st March 1986. A Derby class 108 power-car and trailer DMU takes the single lead for the Colne line at the simplified junction. Immediately in front of the train are points for the double track section to Chaffers Siding but at the end of 1986 the whole of the line to Colne would be reduced to a plain single track with those points removed. (Paul D. Shannon)

BURNLEY BARRACKS

68. Burnley Barracks opened on 18th September 1848 as a temporary terminus as the ELR pushed eastwards. It closed the following February when the line to Bank Top opened but reopened in February 1850. It is on a cramped site, as seen in this L&YR days picture looking up the hill towards Gannow Junction. Above the covered footbridge, a very tall lower quadrant signal can be seen indicating the limited visibility at the station caused by two heavy girder bridges. The girder bridge at the western end had to be rebuilt after July 1960 when a 4F 0-6-0, coming to a stand underneath it, ignited a leaking gas main. (Lancashire & Yorkshire Railway Society)

↑ 69. This 1960s image of Burnley Barracks, from the same viewpoint as picture no. 68, shows the spindly looking footbridge has lost its roofing and the concrete road bridge is now in place. Passing through is Gloucester RC&W Parcels Unit no. M55988. These had a pair of 230hp engines, allowing them to haul a substantial load of parcels vans. M55988 was new to Cricklewood in 1960 but soon transferred to Newton Heath, where it remained until withdrawal in 1980. At this time Burnley Barracks was still well-used by local residents but the 1981 built M65, and associated link roads, cleared many houses and depopulated the area leading to a reduction in passengers. After the line was singled in 1986 all the facilities in view were removed and the surviving up platform is now accessed by a steeply ramped footpath leading to a modern shelter. (Lancashire & Yorkshire Railway Society)

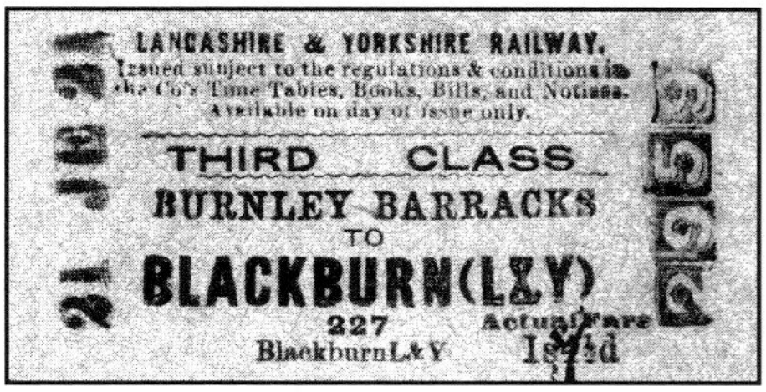

← 70. Looking towards Burnley Central as Sprinter no. 150134 pulls away from Burnley Barracks with a Northern Preston to Colne service on 22nd December 2022. This is now an unstaffed request stop that sees an average of around 500 passengers per week. Just beyond the train, by the end of the platform, the line crosses the Leeds and Liverpool Canal and then runs onto the viaduct that carries the line down to Burnley Central, just two minutes away. (Mark Bartlett)

71. The view along the River Calder as Northern Pacer no. 142020 passes over the 15-arch Bank Top Viaduct with the 10.57 Preston to Colne service on 15th November 2018. Freight and passenger services heading west from Burnley in steam days provided a sight and sound show as they lifted their heavy trains, often banked, up towards Gannow Junction. This Pacer was withdrawn in 2019 but then preserved in operational condition at the Waverley Route Heritage Centre at Whitrope Siding. (Martyn Hilbert)

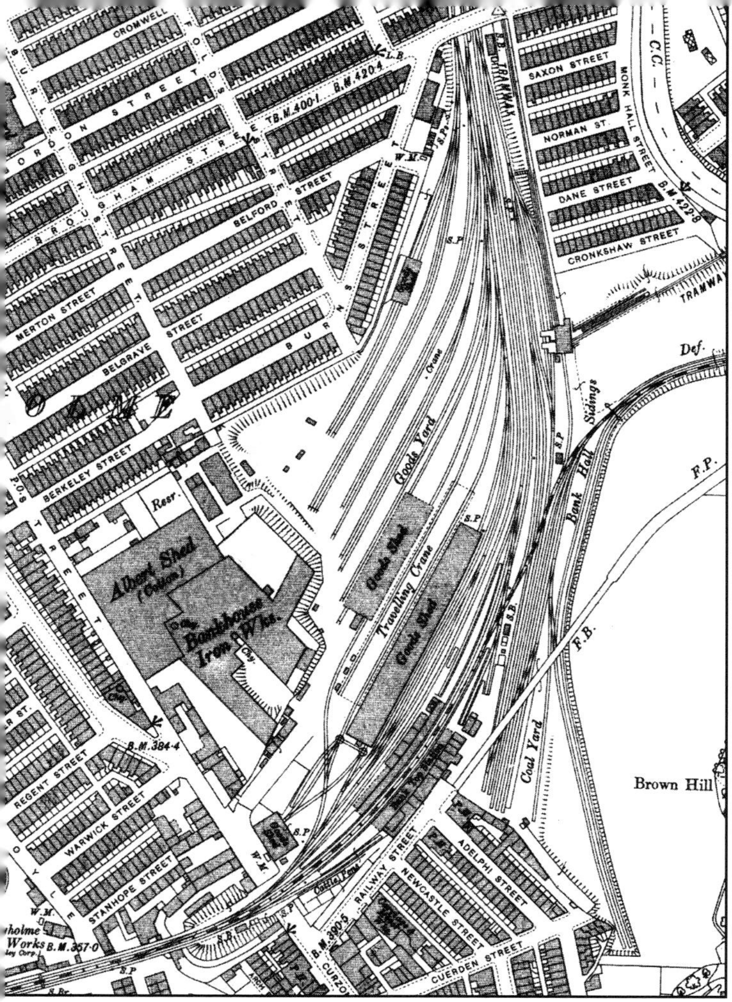

BURNLEY CENTRAL (formerly Bank Top)

XXV. Bank Top station opened as a temporary terminus on 1st December 1848 as the line reached Burnley from Accrington but two months later became a through station as the line to Colne (and Skipton) opened on 1st February 1849. This map extract shows the extensive goods facilities, which were still seeing coal and parcels trains in the late 1970s but are now cleared away with the site built on.

72. An early 1960s picture of Burnley Central (renamed from Bank Top in 1944), from the Blackburn bound platform looking eastwards. The sharp curve prevented freight trains getting a run at the bank up to Gannow Junction, but all passenger trains stopped here (and still do). In 1963 these old canopies and buildings were demolished and replaced by glass fronted, flat roofed structures. (Burnley Civic Trust Heritage Image Collection - bcthic.org)

73. Although the surviving platform at Burnley Central curves sharply there is no compromise by the rigidly angular 1963 station building. The canopy is almost over the tracks at the Colne end but well clear here. Northern Sprinter no. 150108 calls on 22nd December 2022 with a Preston to Colne service. A similar but smaller building on the down platform was demolished after the 1986 singling and nothing remains of the platform, nor indeed the goods and parcels facilities beyond. (Mark Bartlett)

74. Two Derby DMUs leave Burnley Central on 29th March 1986, heading for Colne and passing the site of the exchange sidings for Bank Hall Colliery, closed in 1971. The signal box beyond the station (formerly Burnley Bank Top South) was opened in 1900 and given an extended lever frame in 1931 to allow Bank Top North box to close. The National Carriers parcels depot on the right had closed in the late 1970s, along with the coal concentration depot. With the 1986 singling of the line Burnley Central box closed on 7th December and was soon demolished. There is just a plain track through the shortened single platform today and tree growth restricts most views. (Paul D. Shannon)

Bank Hall Colliery

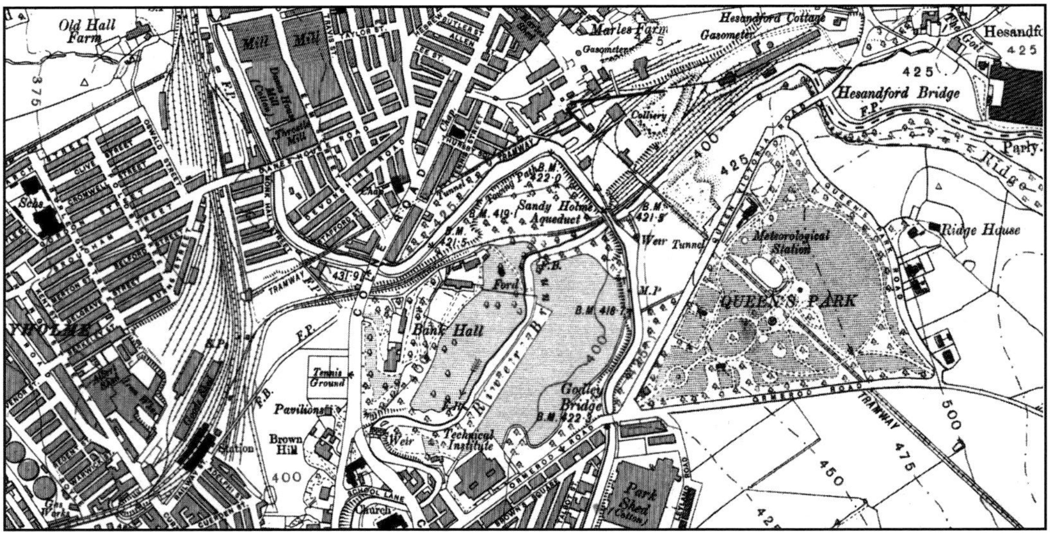

XXVI. Bank Top station had exchange sidings for the large Bank Hall Colliery, reached by a half mile long mineral line. This 6ins to 1 mile 1914 map extract shows the colliery line and also the extensive yards and mineral tramways around the north end of Burnley. Coal from Bank Hall also went out by canal and internal sidings to the wharves can be seen on the map. Burnley Gas Works was also rail served, sited to the west of the main line just off the top of the map.

75. Andrew Barclay 0-4-0ST AB 1448/1919 *King* near the exchange sidings at Burnley, on the half-mile branch from Bank Hall Colliery, on 26th June 1968. It is good that Gordon Edgar took the trouble to capture this industrial scene when the last rites of main line steam were being played out nearby. The 16 tonners appear empty so the loco may be propelling them along the branch towards the pit. Substantial coal trains left here for Lancashire power stations, including Wyre Dock at Fleetwood, and required banking from Burnley Central up to Gannow Junction. Two Barclays worked at Bank Hall, the other being AB 1704/1920 *Carbon* and, unusually, both were fitted with Giesl ejector chimneys. When Bank Hall closed in 1971, *King* was overhauled at NCB Walkden workshops to work on the cliff top lines at Haig Colliery near Whitehaven. (Gordon Edgar)

76. After Bank Hall Colliery closed the associated railway was lifted but can be walked as a surfaced path from Burnley Central station, through Thompson Park with its extensive miniature railway, to the now landscaped pit site beyond the canal aqueduct. Several bridges and other railway features can still be seen on the way and the canal wharves at Bank Hall can also be seen across from the canal towpath. (Mark Bartlett)

Burnley Gas Works

77. Burnley Gas Works was sited on the west side of the line to the north of Bank Top station. For many years the sidings were shunted by a Barclay 0-4-0ST, Burnley Corporation Gas Works (later North Western Gas Board) *No.1*. Its works number was perhaps unique, being AB 1927/1927, the latter number denoting the year of build. The Barclay is shown at the gas works in July 1970, shortly before it was donated to the ELRPS at Helmshore becoming their first steam locomotive. It now resides in Bury Transport Museum. (ColourRail.co.uk)

The Railmotor Services

78. Alongside the gas works was New Hall Bridge Halt, first used in 1908 and one of three opened by the L&YR to counteract the loss of traffic to electric trams. Steam railmotor services were inaugurated between Burnley and Colne in 1906 using two Kerr, Stuart vehicles, one seen here at Colne between services. These curious machines had two boilers and the cylinders only drove the front axle so, with unconnected rear wheels, they were effectively an 0-2-2. The roof boards proclaim 'Burnley Bank Top, Nelson and Colne', and there are retractable steps at each end of the carriage. They had been introduced on the Holcombe Brook branch the previous year but must have struggled on its steep gradients. They were not successful here either and were withdrawn in 1909 but the service continued with L&YR built railmotors, with a second trailer coach. Later, several services each day ran through to Rose Grove. (John Alsop collection)

An extract from the 1914 Bradshaw timetable, the last published before WWI, Manchester to Skipton illustrates the joint working of services through Colne between the L&YR and the Midland.

The lower table shows the railmotor services, introduced eight years earlier, which supplemented the main line trains between Burnley and Colne. (Lancashire and Yorkshire Railway Society)

MANCHESTER, BURY, RAMSBOTTOM, HASLINGDEN, ACCRINGTON, BURNLEY, COLNE, and SKIPTON.—L. & Y.

Miles	Down.		mrn	mrn (One class only.)	mrn	mrn	mrn	mrn	mrn (Through Train, Blackpool (Central) to Colne.)	mrn	mrn	mrn	mrn (Through Train, Manchester to Ilkley.)
	Victoria Station, Manchester	dep.	....	....	5 16	....	....	....		7 12	7 45	....	8 40
¾	Salford		....	....	....	....	5 17	....		7 15	....	8 0	....
2¼	Pendleton		....	....	....	....	5 21	....		7 20	....	8 4	8 47
4¼	Clifton Junction		....	....	....	....	5k41	....		7 25	....	8 9	....
5½	Molyneux Brow		....	....	....	....	....	....		....	....	8 12	....
7	Ringley Road		....	....	....	....	5 47	....		7 31	....	8 17	....
7¾	Radcliffe Bridge		....	....	....	....	5 50	....		7 34	....	8 20	....
10½	Bury (Bolton Street) 794, 809	arr.	....	....	5 37	....	5 55	....		7 39	8 9	8 25	9 1
		dep.	....	....	5 40	....	....	....		7 41		8 26	9 3
13	Summerseat		....	....	5 46	....	....	....		7 47		....	....
14½	Ramsbottom	arr.	....	....	5 49	....	....	....		7 51	Stop	8 34	9 11
—	815 Bacup	dep.	....	....	5 25	....	....	....		7 0	....	7 48	8 38
—	Ramsbottom	dep.	....		5 53	....	....	....		7 53	....	8 35	9 13
17¼	Helmshore		....		6 0	....	....	....		8 0	....	8 42	9 20
19¼	Haslingden		....		6 11	....	....	....		8 6	....	8 48	9 25
20½	Baxenden		....		6 19	....	....	....		8 10	....	8 52	9 31
22¾	Accrington 790	arr.	....		6 27	....	....	....		8 15	mrn	8 57	9 36
		dep.	5 7		6 37	....	....	....		....	9 5	....	9 42
24¼	Huncoat		5 11		6 41	....	....	....		....	9 9	....	....
25¾	Hapton		5 15		6 45	....	....	....		....	9 13	....	....
27½	Rose Grove 786, 821		5 20		6 49	6 59	....	8 20	8 50	....	9 18	....	....
28¼	Burnley Barracks		5 24	6 4	6 55	7 2	....	8 23	8 53	....	9 21	....	....
29	Burnley (Bank Top)		5 26	6 8	6 57	7 8	....	8 29	8 55	....	9 23	....	9 51
31	Brierfield		5 35	6 15	7 9	7 18	....	8 36	9 2	....	9 31	....	10 0
32½	Nelson		5 38	6 19	7 12	7 21	....	8 39	9 6	....	9 35	....	10 3
34¼	Colne	arr.	5 46	6 25	7 21	....	....	8 47	9 13	....	9 42	....	1012
45½	Skipton 656, 658, 665	"	6 35	7 45	8 11	....	....	9 23	....	....	1022	....	1040

Down. (Week Days)		mrn (One class only.)	mrn	mrn	mrn	mrn (Sats. only.)	aft (Sats. only.)	aft	aft (Saturdays only.)	aft	aft	aft	aft (Saturdays only.)	aft	aft (Thro' from London (Euston). Via Bolton and Blackburn.)	aft (Saturdays only.)	aft (Saturdays only.)	aft (Except Saturdays.)	aft (Sats. only.)	aft (Except Saturdays.)
Manchester	dep.	....	9 28	....	1040	1140	....	....	....	1215	....	1 8	....	2 15	2 30	....	....	3 20	3 28	....
Salford		....	....	....	1043		12 5	....	....	1218	....	....	1 15	....		2 38	....			3 40
Pendleton		....	....	....	1047			....	....	1222	....	....	1c20	....		2 42	....			3c44
Clifton Junction		....	....	....	1052			....	....	1227	....	....	1 25	....		2 46	....			3 49
Molyneux Brow		....	....	....	1055			....	....	1230	....	....	1 28	....		2 49	....			3 52
Ringley Road		....	....	....	11 0			....	....	1235	....	....	1 33	....		2 55	....			3 57
Radcliffe Bridge		....	....	....	11 4			....	....	1238	....	....	1 37	....		2 59	....			4 0
Bury (Bolton Street)	arr.	....	9 46	....	11 9	1210	1220	....	....	1243	....	1 40	1 44	2 33		3 5	....	3 38	3 46	4 5
	dep.	....	9 48	....	1113		1221	....	....	1246	....		1 46	2 35			....	3 39	3 47	
Summerseat		....	....	....	1119	....	....	....	....	1252	....	....	1 52	....			....	....	....	
Ramsbottom	arr.		9 56	....	1122	....	1228	....	....	1255	....	....	1 55	2 43			....	3 47	3 54	
815 Bacup	dep.		9 10	....	1055	....	1145n			1230	....	....	1 25	2 10				2 55	2 55	
Ramsbottom	dep.		9 58	....	1125	....	1229	....		1 0	....	....	1 56	2 44				3 48	3 55	
Helmshore			10 5	....	1133	....	1236	....		1 7	....	....	2 3	2 51				3 56	4 2	
Haslingden			1011	....	1140	....	1243	....		1 15	....	....	2 9	2 58				4 3	4 8	
Baxenden			1015	....	1144	....	1247	....		1 21	....	....	2 13	....				4 7	4 12	
Accrington 790	arr.		1020	....	1149	....	1252	....		1 26	....	....	2 18	3 6	3 34			4 12	4 17	....
	dep.	9 47	1022	....	1156	....		1256		1 32	....	....		3 9	3 36			4 15	4 20	....
Huncoat		9 52	....	....	12 0	....	....	1 0		1 36	....	....		3 13	....	....		4 19	4 24	....
Hapton		9 56	....	....	12 4	....	....	1 4		1 40	....	....		3 17	....	....		4 23	4 28	....
Rose Grove 786, 821		10 0	....	1143	12 9	....	....	1 9	1 31	1 44	2 29	....		3 22	h	....		4 28	4 33	....
Burnley Barracks		10 4	1031	1146	1212	....	....	1 12	1 34	1 48	2 32	....		3 25	3 45	....		4 32	4 36	....
Burnley (Bank Top)		1012	1033	1150	1220	....	....	1 14	1 36	1 50	2 34	....		3 27	3 47	....	4 25	4 34	4 38	....
Brierfield		1019	1042	1156	1226	....	....	1 22	1 44	1 59	2 41	....		3 35	3 55	....	4 31	4 42	4 46	....
Nelson		1023	1045	1159	1229	....	....	1 25	1 47	2 2	2 44	....		3 38	3 58	....	4 36	4 45	4 49	....
Colne	arr.	1029	1052	12 6	1238	....	....	1 34	....	2 11	2 52	....		3 47	4 5	....	4 44	4 53	4 56	....
Skipton 656, 658, 665	"	....	1128	1243	1s43	....	....	2s21	....	2 52	....	....		4 19	....	....		5 26	5 26	....

RAIL MOTOR SERVICE—BURNLEY (Bank Top) to COLNE.

(ONE CLASS ONLY.)

		WEEK DAYS.											SUNDAYS.							
		a.m.	a.m.	a.m.	a.m.	p.m.	p.m.	p.m.	p.m.	p.m.	p.m.	p.m.	p.m.	p.m.	p.m.	p.m.	p.m.	p.m.	p.m.	p.m.
BURNLEY (Bank Top)	dep.	6 8	6 55	8 0	10 12	3 0	4 0	5 35	7 15	8 10	9 10	10 28	2 25	3 35	4 35	5 35	6 40	7 26	8 40	9 35
New Hall Bridge (Halt)	"	[illegible]	[illegible]	[illegible]	[illegible]	[illegible]	[illegible]	[illegible]	[illegible]	[illegible]	[illegible]	[illegible]	[illegible]	[illegible]	[illegible]	[illegible]	[illegible]	[illegible]	[illegible]	[illegible]
Reedley Hallows (Halt)	"	[illegible]	[illegible]	[illegible]	[illegible]	[illegible]	[illegible]	[illegible]	[illegible]	[illegible]	[illegible]	[illegible]	[illegible]	[illegible]	[illegible]	[illegible]	[illegible]	[illegible]	[illegible]	[illegible]
Brierfield	"	[illegible]	[illegible]	[illegible]	[illegible]	[illegible]	[illegible]	[illegible]	[illegible]	[illegible]	[illegible]	[illegible]	[illegible]	[illegible]	[illegible]	[illegible]	[illegible]	[illegible]	[illegible]	[illegible]
Nelson	"	[illegible]	[illegible]	[illegible]	[illegible]	[illegible]	[illegible]	[illegible]	[illegible]	[illegible]	[illegible]	[illegible]	[illegible]	[illegible]	[illegible]	[illegible]	[illegible]	[illegible]	[illegible]	[illegible]
Bott Lane (Halt)	"	[illegible]	[illegible]	[illegible]	[illegible]	[illegible]	[illegible]	[illegible]	[illegible]	[illegible]	[illegible]	[illegible]	[illegible]	[illegible]	[illegible]	[illegible]	[illegible]	[illegible]	[illegible]	[illegible]
COLNE	arr.	6 25	7 17	8 17	10 29	3 17	4 17	5 55	7 32	8 27	9 27	10 46	2 42	3 52	4 52	5 52	6 57	7 43	8 57	9 52

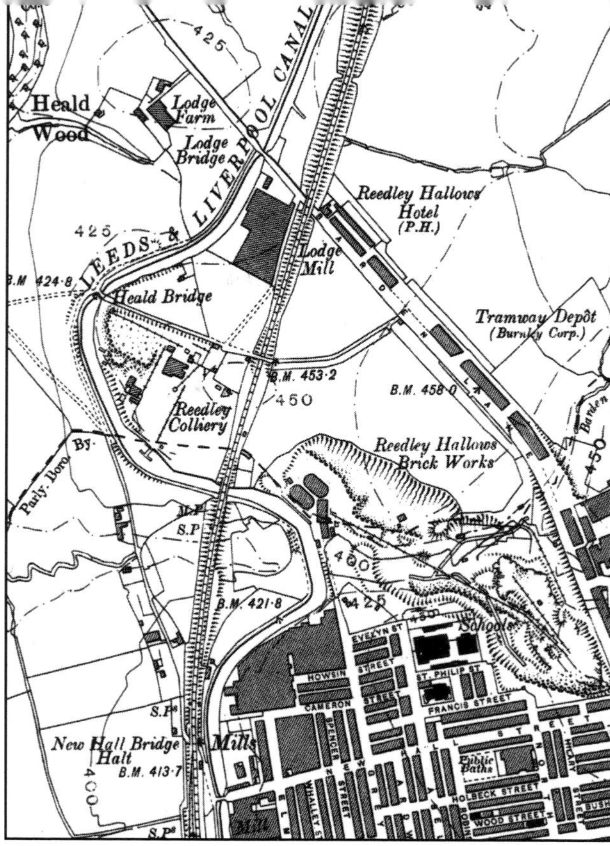

XXVII. This 6ins to 1 mile 1914 map extract shows the location of two of the railmotor halts, at New Hall Bridge and Reedley Hallows. This map predates Burnley Gas Works, which was constructed in the fields alongside New Hall Bridge. Reedley Colliery opened in 1879. It was not rail served but had canal wharves. However, it was connected underground with Bank Hall Colliery in Burnley by 1893 and its output extracted there. It closed in 1960. New Hall Bridge opened on 1st March 1908, built at rail level from old sleepers and the coaches had retractable steps for passengers. The railmotors were later replaced by push-pull trains operated by L&YR 2-4-2Ts, but still with retractable steps. New Hall Bridge closed on 27th September 1948, eight years before push-pull trains ceased but there is no trace of either of the halts today.

79. Another railmotor stop opened on 1st May 1911, known as Reedley Hallows Halt, with two rail level platforms on the embankment. However, this was sited by a main road and lasted until 3rd December 1956. Towards the end of its existence the L&YR 2-4-2Ts were joined on the push-pull services by new BR Standard 2MT 84000 series 2-6-2Ts. Reedley Hallows probably closed as the new DMUs due to be introduced could not service ground level platforms. Sprinter no. 156429 passes the site with a Colne to Preston service on 8th March 2023. (Mark Bartlett)

BRIERFIELD

80. An L&YR era picture of Brierfield station, looking towards Nelson and Colne. It was known as Marsden when opened on 1st February 1849 but renamed in 1857. A 2-4-2T is at the head of a rake of coaches that contains two brake vans with the projecting windows for the guard. Whilst the platform buildings in this image were demolished in the 1970s the lattice footbridge still carries a public footpath across the surviving single track. The signal box lasted until 2014, by which time it was 140 years old. (Lens of Sutton Association)

81. Brierfield looking west on 9th July 2011, with Pacer no. 142016 calling on a Colne to Blackpool South service. The signal box was still operational but with just two signal levers to protect the crossing. It was demolished after closure. Beyond the crossing, on the left, a builders merchant occupies the old goods yard, which closed on 24th April 1967. When the yard was operational it was accessed via points controlled by a separate signal box, sited on the curve in the distance. The crossing barriers are now controlled from Preston Power Box. While many Pacers are preserved, 142016 was scrapped in the European Metal Recycling yard at Kingsbury. (John McIntyre)

82. The 73 yards long Brierfield Tunnel lies just east of the station, taking the line under the A682 road to Nelson. This LMS era picture shows Hughes-Fowler 'Crab' 2-6-0 2705, later 42705, heading west with a train of non-corridor stock. The Crabs were often used on excursion trains from East Lancashire to the coastal resorts, right up to the 1960s when this traffic was lost. No. 42705 was withdrawn from Birkenhead on Boxing Day 1964, after a working life of 38 years and three days, and scrapped by Wards of Sheffield in March 1965. (Lens of Sutton Association)

83. Once Gannow Junction to Colne was singled it became the almost exclusive preserve of Pacer and Sprinter DMUs. However, on 23rd May 1993, Pathfinder Tours 1Z46 'Lancastrian Mini-Excursions' railtour visited as part of a two day event covering many North West lines, including the Padiham branch. Two BRCW class 26s took the train to Colne and no. 60084 *Cross Fell*, new to service only that year, brought it back again. The long train had just passed through Brierfield Tunnel and was approaching the station when photographed. Apart from an occasional Network Rail Measurement Train, it would be 2022 before another loco hauled train visited this line. (Stephen Willetts)

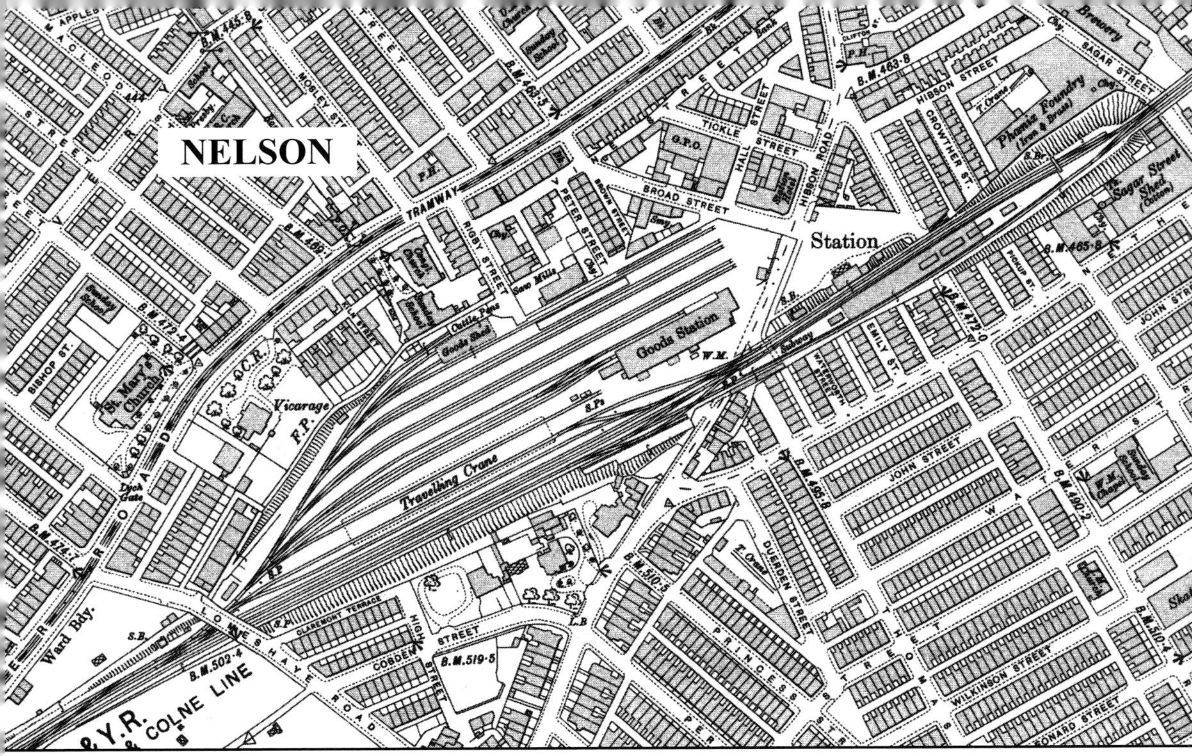

XXVIII. Nelson station opened with the line on 1st February 1849. Initially it had two side platforms but was rebuilt by the L&YR around 1900 with their favoured island platform style. This was similar to that at Rose Grove but whereas that station was accessed down from a road overbridge Nelson had a ramp up from a subway. The extensive general goods yard shown here closed on 26th April 1965 and the site is now commercial and retail premises.

84. This L&YR days photograph shows the post-1900 station at Nelson, with activity around the frontage and a crowded platform. A present day view would be of what is now known as Nelson Interchange, with bus services operating from the old station forecourt. Although the three-storey building has gone, a ticket office is housed in its modern replacement. The canopy has survived on the platform (the last in present day Lancashire), although trains only call at one side of the island on the singled line. Despite the basic hourly service the official recorded passenger numbers at Nelson in 2019-20 were a healthy 121,000. (John Alsop collection)

85. A pair of Derby class 108 DMUs, heading for Colne, call at Nelson on 30th May 1983. At this time the line was still double track and the signal box operational but that would change in 1986. With singling, the track the DMU is on was lifted and the box closed but the island platform retains its L&YR canopy, accessed by a ramp from a subway just beyond this platform building. (Paul D. Shannon)

86. Leaving Nelson towards Colne the railway passes over a low stone viaduct. On 14th September 1981 prototype 2-car railbus no. 140001 was an unusual visitor. This was its first day of operation here, working a diagram alongside the Cravens DMUs. The *Burnley Express* reported that local rail officials believed the new train could be the saviour of the East Lancashire Line, which the production Pacers proved to be. First-time passengers were reported to be impressed with the power operated doors, modern looks and public address system but noted that the train was noisier than the old trains. Station manager, John Balaam, explained that it would be 'a shade more noisy' because it had fixed wheels rather than bogies but he expected the problem to be solved. That complaint did of course dog the Pacers throughout their long life. (Tom Heavyside)

XXIX. One third of a mile from Nelson, travelling towards Colne, Chaffers Siding signal box controlled a level crossing and, until 1930, access to Catlow's stone works.

87. Chaffers was an unremarkable place but in August 1971, after the line to Skipton closed, the two miles from here to Colne were singled and it became the point where the single line staff was handed over and returned. The box had been retained to supervise the level crossing on Barkerhouse Road, which is busy and steeply graded. On 14th September 1981 a Cravens DMU leaves the double track section. This view was from the footbridge, which obscured the view of the road from the box, hence the mirror mounted to the left of the gate post. (Tom Heavyside)

88. On 7th December 1986 the remaining route from Gannow Junction to Chaffers Siding was singled and after 15 years of controlling the single line the signal box was reduced to the status of 'Gate Box', with just two semaphores to protect the crossing. Just before this change Pacer no. 142038, making its way from Colne to Preston, pauses to hand over the single line staff. Another railwayman is waiting to open the gates, manually operated by this time rather than by the box hand wheel. For just over four years, trains would now be able to hurry over Barkerhouse Road without stopping. (Stephen Willetts)

89. On 20th March 1991 the Chaffers Siding signal box finally closed and it and the adjoining footbridge were demolished. A possibly unique situation for a passenger line then ensued whereby, on either side of the crossing, a train man operated switch was installed. Drivers pulled up alongside the board shown in the inset and pulled the cord to operate the lights and barriers. Once the barriers were down a light illuminated and the driver then made the decision whether the train could safely proceed. Barriers would rise automatically after the train had passed. (John McIntyre)

90. After years of ‘pulling the cord’, in September 2014 treadles were installed that switch on the crossing lights and lower the barriers, saving perhaps one minute of waiting. However, such is the nature of this steep road, trains still have to halt and await the light authorisation to proceed slowly at the driver’s discretion. On 22nd November 2023, Sprinter no. 156409 is on the move again heading for Preston after pausing to ensure it was safe to pass over Barkerhouse Road. If the Colne to Skipton route reopens to through services, including freight trains, a different system will certainly be needed here. (Mark Bartlett)

Nelson Mineral Yard

XXX. Nelson Mineral Yard opened in 1904, to the east of Chaffers Siding, and supplemented the general goods facilities provided in the yard by Nelson station.

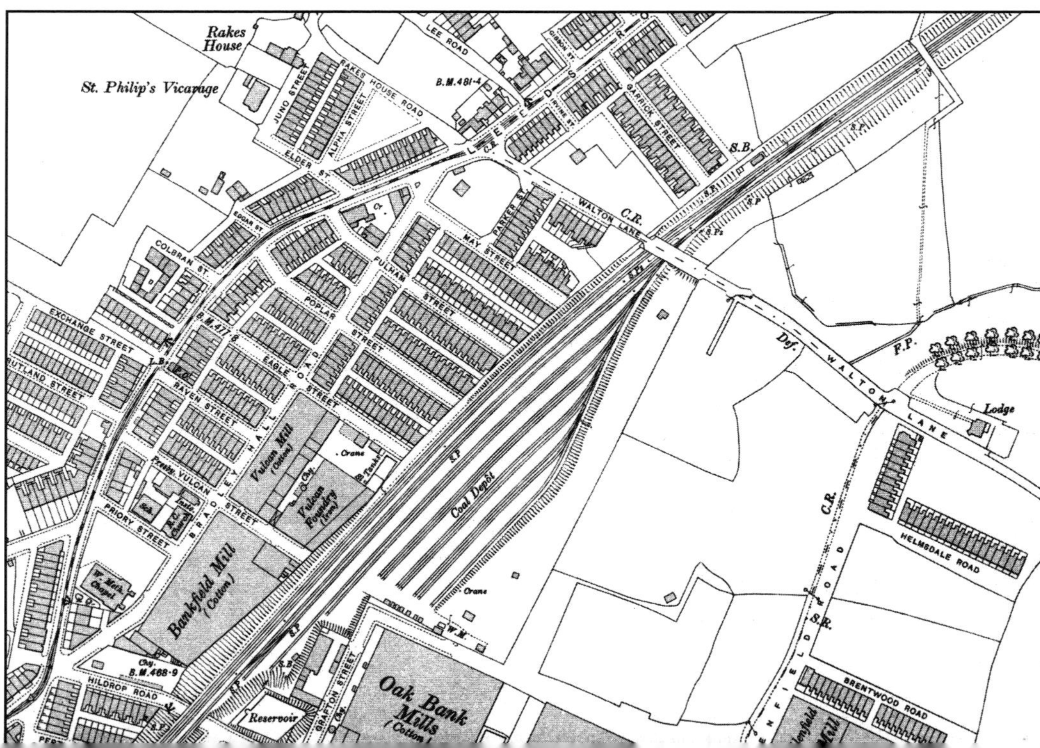

91. This view looks southwest from a footbridge overlooking the headshunt of the yard with Nelson Mineral Yard signal box visible on the right. The yard was later designated a Coal Concentration Depot but closed on 27th March 1976. (Lancashire and Yorkshire Railway Society)

Bott Lane Halt

92. Continuing towards Colne, Bott Lane was another ground level railmotor halt, built from sleepers, with a small shelter. There isn't actually a Bott Lane, the road leading to it being Bott House Lane but it is often shortened. It opened in 1906 and, like Reedley Hallows, lasted until 1956 when push-pull services were withdrawn, just ahead of DMU introduction. Ironically, there have been developments since closure, including Pendle Community College and a large high school, all of which would have contributed traffic. In this view, looking northeast from the same footbridge as the image above, an unidentified Stanier Black 5 trundles a freight towards Colne. Bott House Lane can be seen beyond the field above the locomotive. The halt was sited where the lane meets the railway but nothing remains today other than an emergency access point. (Lancashire and Yorkshire Railway Society)

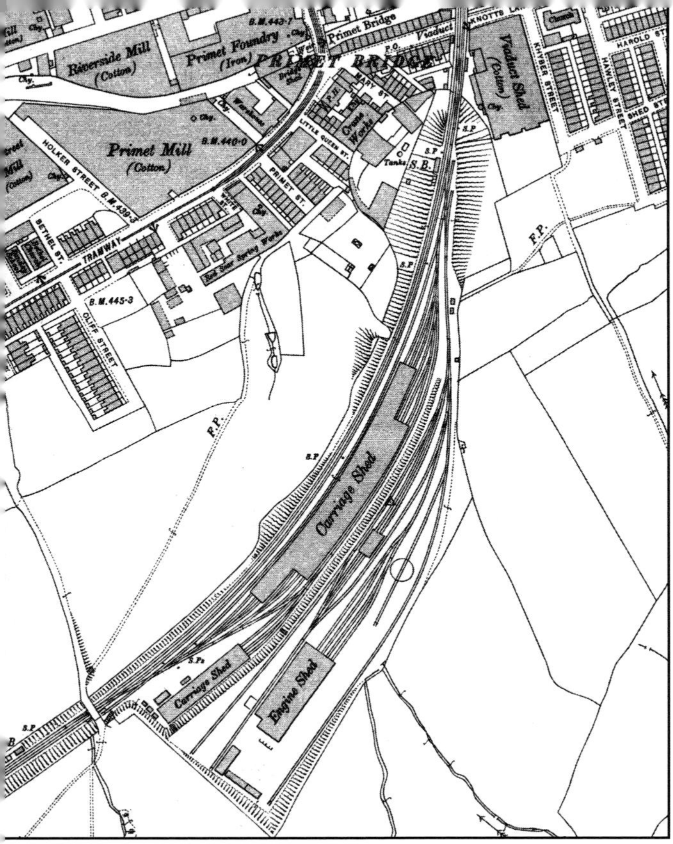

Colne Shed and Carriage Sidings/Depot

XXXI. Colne engine shed was opened by the L&YR in 1900 after they ceased sharing facilities with the Midland Railway. It closed in 1936 when its locomotives and staff were transferred to Rose Grove. Although the shed was demolished, the old turntable was retained for use by engines taking coaches to or from the adjacent carriage sidings. This large depot was kept busy right through to the 1960s, and indeed a new staff amenity block was constructed in 1959. Many excursions and service trains started at Colne because of the carriage servicing there. Things quickly changed with the publication of the Beeching Report and the demise of summer excursion traffic. That, combined with the loss of long distance services and the introduction of DMUs, meant that the depot closed in 1967 and was demolished soon after.

93. Black 5s nos 45261 and 45437 double-head the 21.03 Wakes Week excursion 1E33 to Great Yarmouth via the Woodhead route, just beginning its overnight journey from Colne on 30th June 1967. This was the third of five holiday trains leaving that evening but this sort of traffic was really winding down by this time. Viewed from the Wackersall Road bridge, the large carriage servicing sheds are visible behind the train, with the modern staff amenity building on the right, all to be abandoned later that year. (Cliff Bancroft)

94. A 2023 view from Wackersall Road, showing the area once occupied by the carriage depot and sidings. After the 1967 closure the large site was unused for many years but is now covered by housing. Northern Sprinter no. 156406 is moments into its journey from Colne to Preston on 22nd November as it rounds the curve on the line that was singled in 1971. Sixty years earlier the sidings on either side of the running lines would have been occupied by long rakes of stock that had been used on the summer excursions but would be idle over the winter period. (Mark Bartlett)

95. Between the carriage sidings and the station is the six arch viaduct over the valley of the Colne Water. This imposing structure still dominates the west side of the town. In April 1960 Stanier 4MT 2-6-4T no. 42460, allocated to 26D Bury MPD, rolls across the viaduct towards the station with a passenger service that has probably travelled via the Stubbins to Accrington line then on through Burnley to terminate here. (G. Warnes courtesy ColourRail.co.uk)

COLNE

XXXII. Colne station was opened in October 1848 by the Leeds and Bradford Extension Railway, later to become part of the Midland Railway. After some slight delays the L&YR arrived in the town in February 1849. Right from the outset there was an amicable working arrangement between the two companies who made an end on junction in the single station with through trains. In the 19th century the Midland even allowed the L&YR engines to be serviced at their shed in the town but from 1900 they each had their own shed. The Midland shed is at the top left of this map extract but it closed in 1936 when the duties and staff were transferred to Skipton. There was also a substantial goods yard alongside the station and this generated traffic right through to the late 1960s.

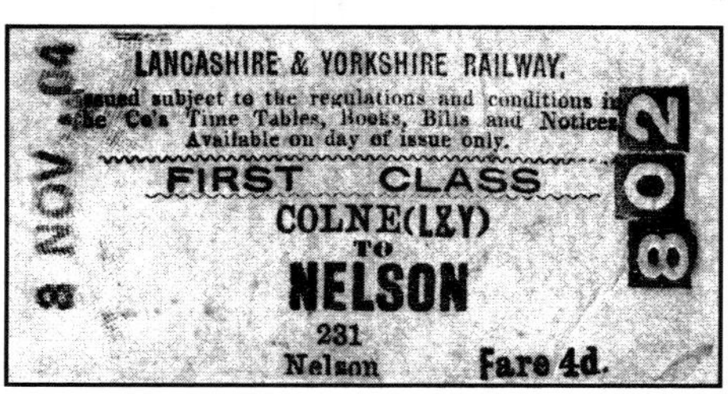

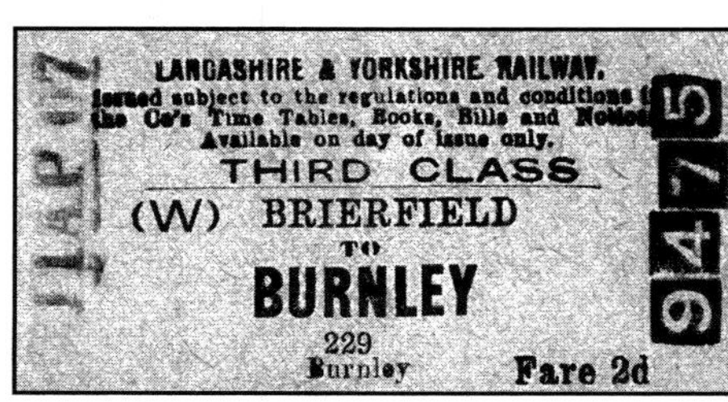

96. This Edwardian postcard shows the Colne station buildings, which lasted until the closure of the Skipton route in 1970, and a tram climbing Primet Hill towards the town centre, passing under the bridge that still carries the line today. The station forecourt shown here still acts as a small car park for the station. (John Alsop collection)

97. Although Colne was designed as a through station from the outset, it was a joint facility where the L&YR and Midland met. There was some through running but many services started and terminated there. In this pre-grouping image, looking towards the viaduct, a Midland Railway 4-4-0 is in the bay platform before departing towards Skipton and is probably awaiting a connecting L&YR train from Manchester or Preston. (Lens of Sutton Association)

98. The much reduced Colne station on 1st March 1986, with a Birmingham RCW class 104 two-car DMU awaiting departure for Preston. The buildings seen in picture 97 were demolished in 1971 after Colne became a terminus and 15 years on the basic halt is unchanged. (Paul D. Shannon)

99. Colne epitomises the decline of many railways post Beeching. The original layout is shown in map XXXII, on the previous page, but after the 1970 closure of the Skipton line the station was reduced to this single platform with a small shelter. Taken from a similar spot to the Midland Railway picture, this is a Colne to Preston service with Pacer no. 142062 on 4th March 1988. Beyond the viaduct the cleared area of Colne carriage depot follows the curving line towards Burnley, since used for housing. Since 1971 there have been various shelters, and the latest has a ticket issuing machine, but the scene is otherwise unchanged, apart from significant tree growth. (Tom Heavyside).

FOULRIDGE

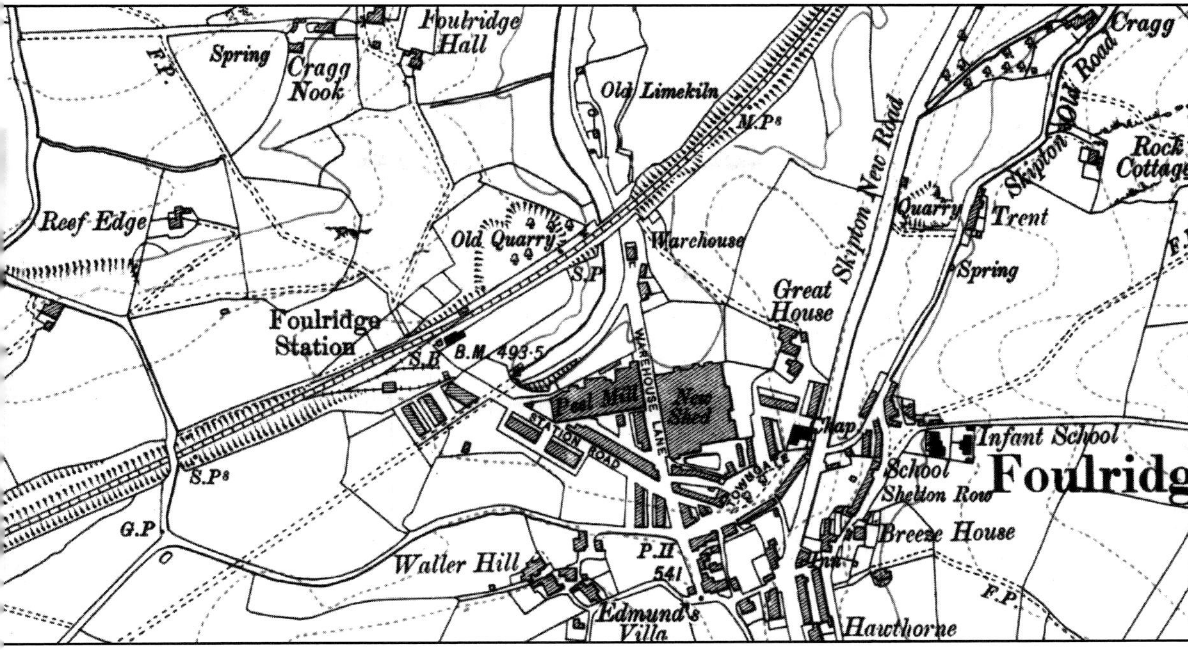

XXXIII. Foulridge, just over two miles from Colne, opened with the line on 2nd October 1848. As can be seen, it was on the outskirts of the village. The main Skipton to Colne road passes through the village centre which made the station vulnerable to bus competition and it closed on 5th January 1959. This 1915 6ins map extract also shows the Leeds and Liverpool canal entering the village via the mile-long Foulridge Tunnel and then passing under the line. The girder bridge that carried the railway over it was dismantled after the 1970 closure and will need to be replaced if the line reopens.

100. An early postcard of Foulridge, looking generally southeastwards from the outskirts of the village with the station in the foreground. The small goods yard is just off picture to the right but this closed at the same time as passenger services ceased. Trains continued to pass through until 1970 and the station building remained in place on the platforms, gradually deteriorating, until 1986. (John Alsop collection)

101. The stone Midland Railway station building at Foulridge was fortunate to survive into the 1980s as it then became a candidate for preservation. The Keighley and Worth Valley railway had been operating their heritage branch line since 1968 and now wanted to construct a proper station at Ingrow West, where the old building had had to be demolished. Foulridge was dismantled stone by stone and transported the relatively short distance to Ingrow to be rebuilt and now sees regular heritage services again. It has a real period feel, as seen in this 2019 view, and that continues into the offices and public areas inside the building. (David Bosher)

Barnoldswick Junction

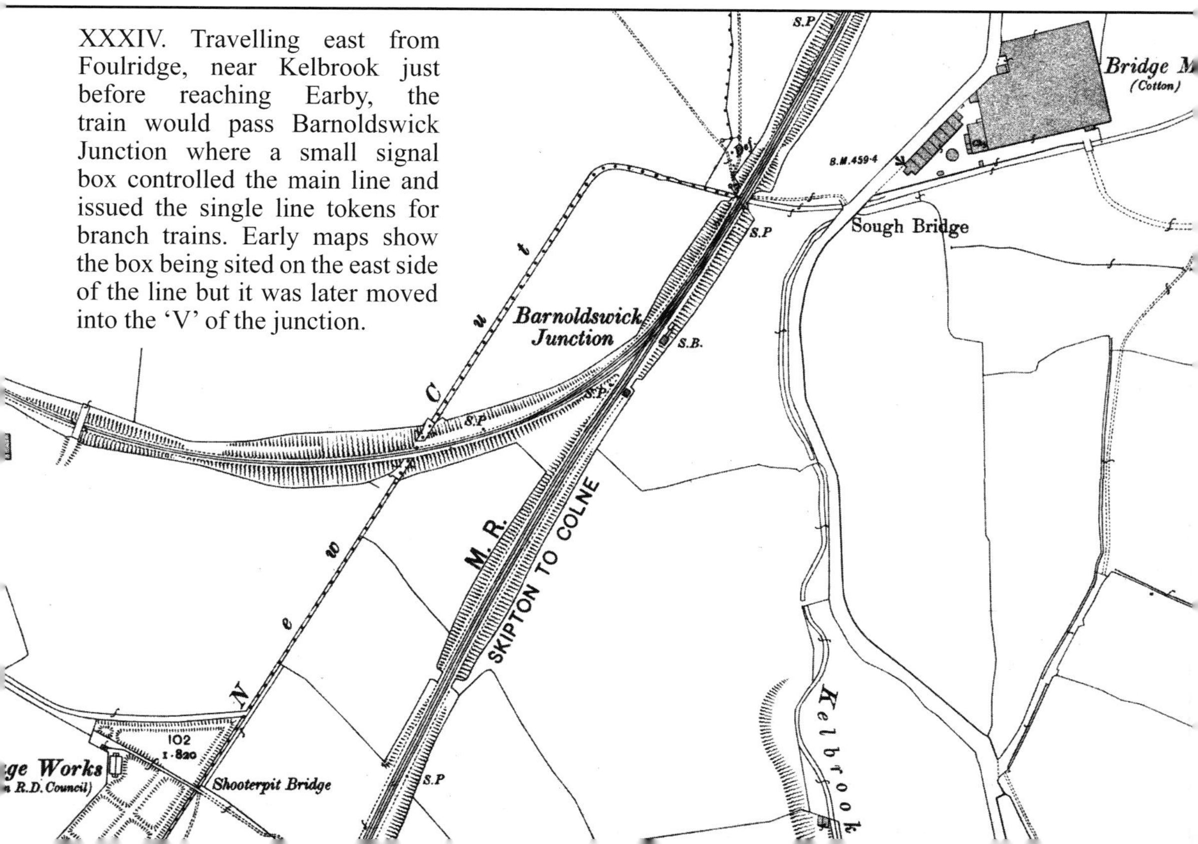

XXXIV. Travelling east from Foulridge, near Kelbrook just before reaching Earby, the train would pass Barnoldswick Junction where a small signal box controlled the main line and issued the single line tokens for branch trains. Early maps show the box being sited on the east side of the line but it was later moved into the 'V' of the junction.

102. Barnoldswick Junction in September 1955, with the single line token being handed over as the driver leans out of the push-pull coach, heading towards Earby. At this time there were still 12 branch passenger trains each day but the following year that was reduced to just two, which continued until 1965. The box was operational until the last goods train left the branch on 1st August 1966, but then stood disused until the 1970 main line closure. Almost 60 years after the last signal lever was pulled, the concrete base of the box and some associated steelwork is still lying in the undergrowth. Although Barnoldswick has strong links with Colne and East Lancashire there was never a triangular junction here and all branch trains ran towards Earby and Skipton. (Lens of Sutton Association/Robert Kirkland coll.)

EARBY

XXXV. Earby station opened with the line in October 1848, and closed with it in February 1970. It was the junction station for Barnoldswick until 1965. There was a level crossing at the station, and another at the Skipton end of the village controlled by a separate signal box. The goods shed survives but all other railway infrastructure has been dismantled since closure.

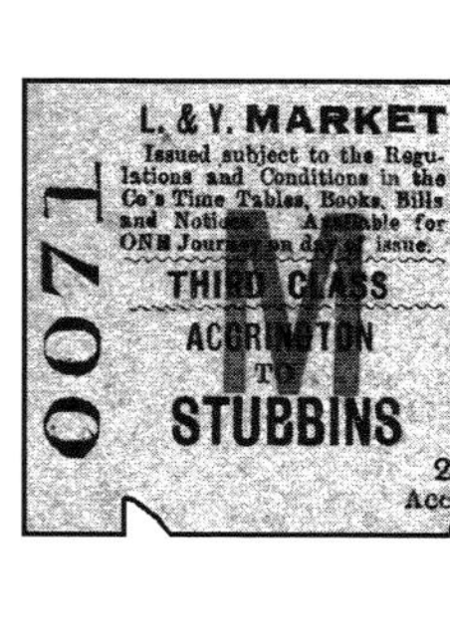
L. & Y. MARKET
Issued subject to the Regulations and Conditions in the Co's Time Tables, Books, Bills and Notices. Available for ONE Journey on day of issue.
THIRD CLASS
ACCRINGTON
TO
STUBBINS
0071
M
2

103. This is a Midland Railway days' picture of Earby, from the Salterforth Road level crossing, looking towards Skipton. The loop platform for Barnoldswick trains was to the right of the platform building. The goods shed can be seen in the distance, and survives in use as a garage. The footbridge extended across all the tracks. Although the road is narrow the crossing gates had to protect three tracks and so were much wider than might be expected. (Paul Laming collection)

104. Earby loop platform on Saturday 17th June 1961, with push-pull fitted Ivatt 2MT 2-6-2T no. 41327 waiting to take the 11.52am SO service to Barnoldswick. By this date there were just two trains a day on the branch, run for the benefit of pupils attending school in Skipton. Therefore, on Saturdays the second train ran at lunchtime rather than later in the afternoon. This basic service continued until closure in 1965, latterly with DMUs on the second train of the day.
(R Patterson courtesy ColourRail.co.uk)

105. All appears as normal looking west from Earby towards Barnoldswick Junction and Colne, but it is 1971 and the line to Colne closed in February 1970 so the station and signal box are waiting for the demolition gang. Before it all goes though there are items of interest, not least the lower quadrant signal mounted under the footbridge. The Barnoldswick branch trains ran from the other side of this island platform, but that loop line was lifted after the 1965 closure and only plain track is in view now. However, because there were once three tracks, the level crossing gates here covered a wide expanse of railway land. Salterforth Road however was narrow and the gates can be seen to be closed across open trackwork rather than crossing boards. Equally, when the gates were open for trains to pass only a small section of one on each side blocked the roadway. (Michelle J Howe)

6. The Barnoldswick Branch

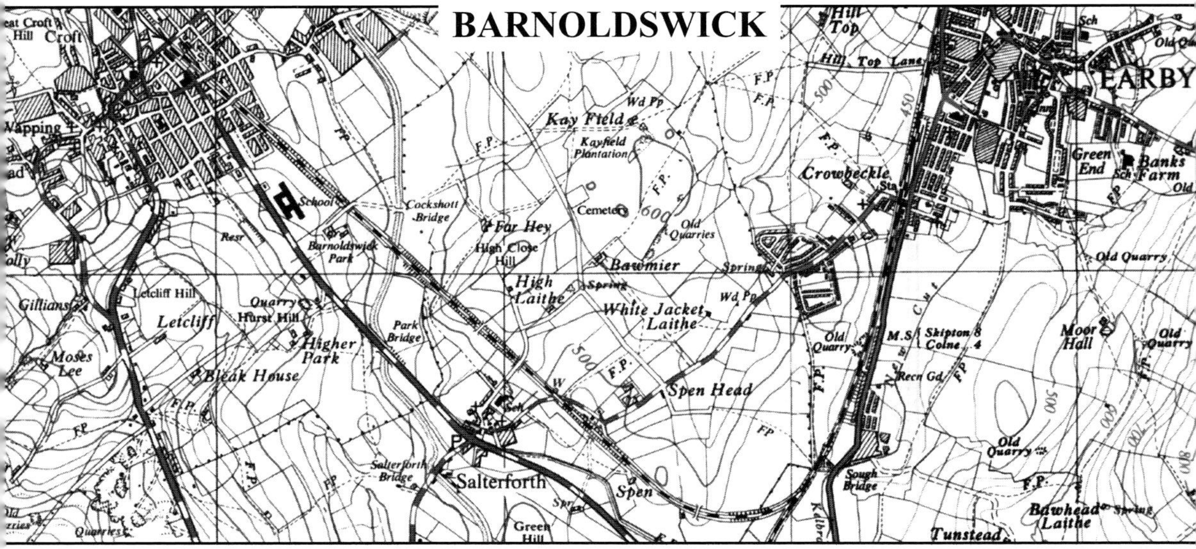

XXXVI. In 1846, the BC&NWJR proposed to build a line that would pass through Barnoldswick but it was not started. Similarly, the FP&WRJR had grand plans to link from the Longridge Railway through the Ribble Valley and Barnoldswick to join the Colne to Skipton line near Elslack. After building a short section to link the Longridge line to the rest of the network nothing more was heard of the scheme. Business people in Barnoldswick became frustrated by these failed plans and promoted the independent Barnoldswick Railway Company, which was authorised by Parliament on 12th August 1865. Construction works started in 1867 and the 1¾ mile branch opened on 8th February 1871. This 1937 2½ ins to 1 mile map extract shows the full length of the branch and most of the main line into Earby.

106. The Barnoldswick branch was worked by the Midland Railway on behalf of the owners from the outset. Because the goods yard was beyond the passenger station there was a through platform and in 1896 there was a further proposal for a light railway to connect with the L&YR at Gisburn. The L&YR would not allow the connection and the scheme did not proceed. In 1899 the Midland took ownership of the line. In this turn of the century postcard one of their 0-6-0Ts is seen in the platform. Three very different buildings appear to have been joined together to provide the station facilities. (Lens of Sutton Association)

107. 'Barlick' is a common abbreviation for Barnoldswick and from the earliest days the branch train was known as the 'Barlick Spud', apparently because the first locomotive was so small it was likened to a portable potato roaster. This became the local nickname for all trains throughout the branch's life. Push-pull fitted Ivatt 2MT 2-6-2T no. 41273 stands in the single platform before propelling its train back to Earby in September 1955. After the 1966 final closure this area was cleared and the only building to survive is the old station house on Fernlea Avenue, now the Station House Dental Practice. (Lens of Sutton Association/Robert Kirkland collection)

108. One much photographed feature of Barnoldswick station was the ancient crossbar signal. This protected the level crossing but when open to rail traffic the red bar could be turned through 90 degrees. In the early days of the railway there was also a small single road engine shed in the yard to house the branch engine. The left-hand picture shows the signal, Wellhouse Road level crossing and part of the goods yard beyond. The right-hand picture is a direct 'then and now' comparison as the war memorial was re-sited to the area between Wellhouse Road and the new car park after the railway closed. (*left:* Lens of Sutton Association/John Faulkner coll.; *right:* Mark Bartlett)

109. Most of the infrastructure of this short line has disappeared since closure. The goods yard has become a public open space and the station a car park and supermarket. Beyond that the course of the line can be seen as a space between buildings but occupied by allotments and parking spaces. Moving out into open country the course is less clear but a substantial abutment of the bridge over the Leeds and Liverpool Canal remains on the south side, and looks like it will be there for some time. On the north side of the canal a marina has been opened and the other abutment and its adjacent embankment have been removed. Continuing south the trackbed only really becomes visible again as the curve of the line towards Barnoldswick Junction commences. (Mark Bartlett)

Calling the Barnoldswick service from 1956 to 1965 'sparse' doesn't really convey the situation. This is an extract from the London Midland timetable of 1964. The steam push-pull worked in empty before heading for Skipton at 8.19am. On weekdays a DMU from Skipton arrived at 4.49pm and returned there at 5.00pm. On Saturdays, reflecting that Skipton Grammar School had morning classes, a train arrived from Earby at 11.52am, but left empty stock – and that was it.

Table 152—

BARNOLDSWICK AND EARBY
WEEKDAYS ONLY

Miles		C a.m.		C SX p.m.								
0	BARNOLDSWICK ....dep	8 19	•	5 0	•	•	•	•	•	•	•	•
2¼	EARBY ....arr	8 25	...	5 6	...	...	...	...	...	...	...	...
Miles		SO a.m.		B SX p.m.								
0	EARBY ....dep	11 45	•	4 42	•	•	•	•	•	•	•	•
2¼	BARNOLDSWICK ....arr	11 52	...	4 49	...	...	...	...	...	...	...	...

B—Through Carriage from Skipton.
C—Through Carriage to Skipton.
SO—Saturdays only.
SX—Saturdays excepted.

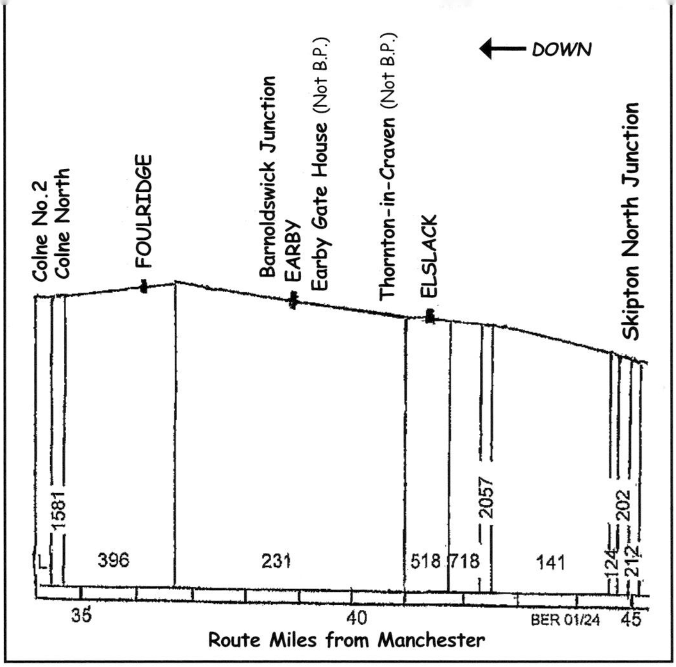

7. Onwards to Skipton

← *Gradient profile from Colne through to Skipton.*

110. Half a mile east of Earby station the line passed another level crossing, over the main Colne to Skipton road. On 28th July 1968 another 'End of Steam Special' approaches the crossing hauled by Black 5s nos. 45073 and 45156. The crossing originally had its own full-size Midland Railway signal box but in later years that was replaced by a much smaller cabin, perhaps working under the supervision of Earby station box. This small structure was another one snapped up by the Keighley and Worth Valley Railway after closure and they installed it on tiny Damems station. Apart from some roller shutter housings at gutter level it looks much as it did when in use at Earby.
(Mike Taylor and David Bosher)

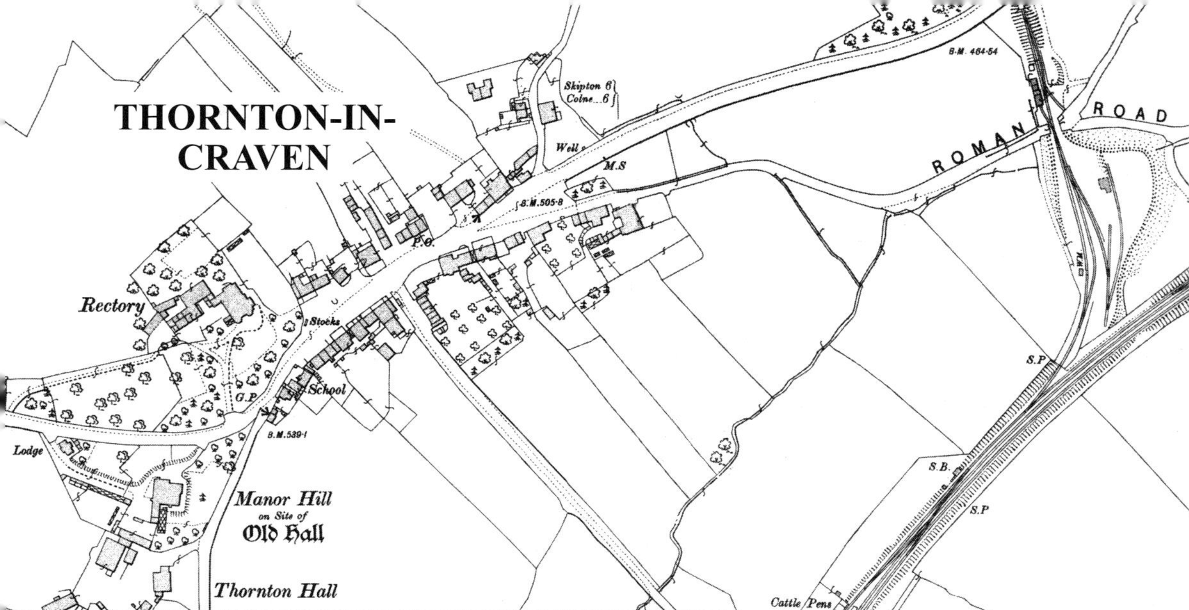

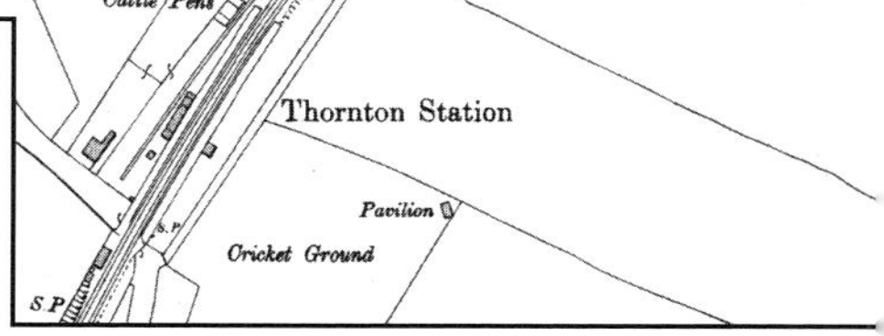

XXXVII. Just over a mile to the north-east of Earby station, Thornton station opened in October 1848. The "–in-Craven" was officially added in 1937, although it had been used informally for many years prior to that. It was sited a quarter of a mile from the small village, at the bottom of a steep hill on a country lane, so regular buses between Colne and Skipton, passing through the village centre, later took away much of its business. The goods siding closed as early as 1951, and from 1959 onwards the station was threatened with closure to passengers on several occasions but managed to remain open until closed with the line in 1970.

111. Newly preserved Gresley K4 2-6-0 no.3442 *The Great Marquess* passes through Thornton-in-Craven with 'The Dalesman' RCTS railtour on 4th May 1963. This started in Bradford and visited the Ilkley to Embsay line and the Grassington branch before passing through here on its way to Barnoldswick. It later also visited Padiham. The station is looking run-down but was still staffed at this time and would remain open for another seven years. The buildings were demolished after closure but the down platform is still substantially complete, although heavily overgrown. If the long campaign to reopen the line comes to fruition a double track line will reappear, presumably with electrification masts too, but the station itself is unlikely to reopen. A new station at Earby, serving Barnoldswick and the surrounding area, seems more practical. (Colour Rail)

Thornton Quarry and Limestone Works branch

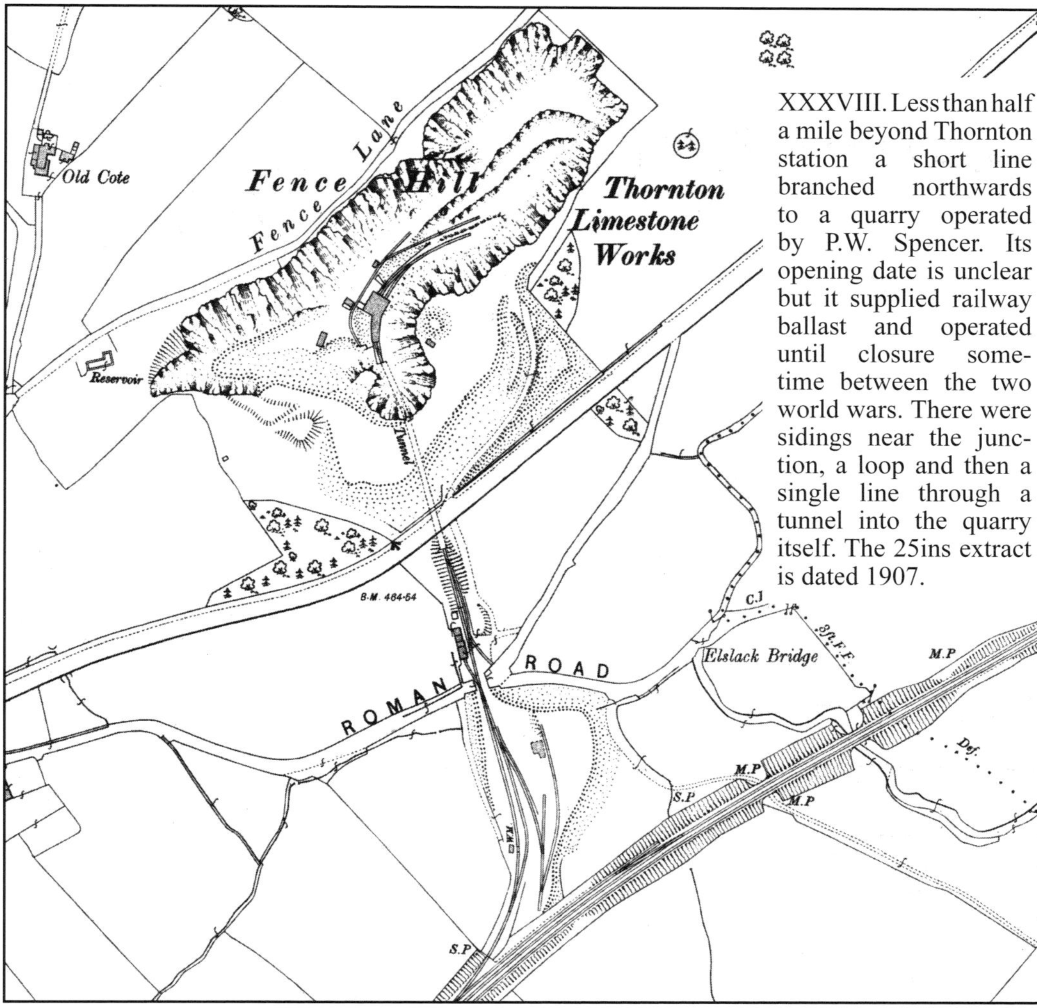

XXXVIII. Less than half a mile beyond Thornton station a short line branched northwards to a quarry operated by P.W. Spencer. Its opening date is unclear but it supplied railway ballast and operated until closure sometime between the two world wars. There were sidings near the junction, a loop and then a single line through a tunnel into the quarry itself. The 25ins extract is dated 1907.

112. Surprisingly, considering it has been closed for around a century, much remains of the short Thornton Quarry branch including this stone bridge over Old Road, seen in October 2023. On the branch, after this bridge, the old tunnel can still be seen although the quarry is now part flooded and after heavy rain it drains through the tunnel and along the trackbed. (Mark Bartlett)

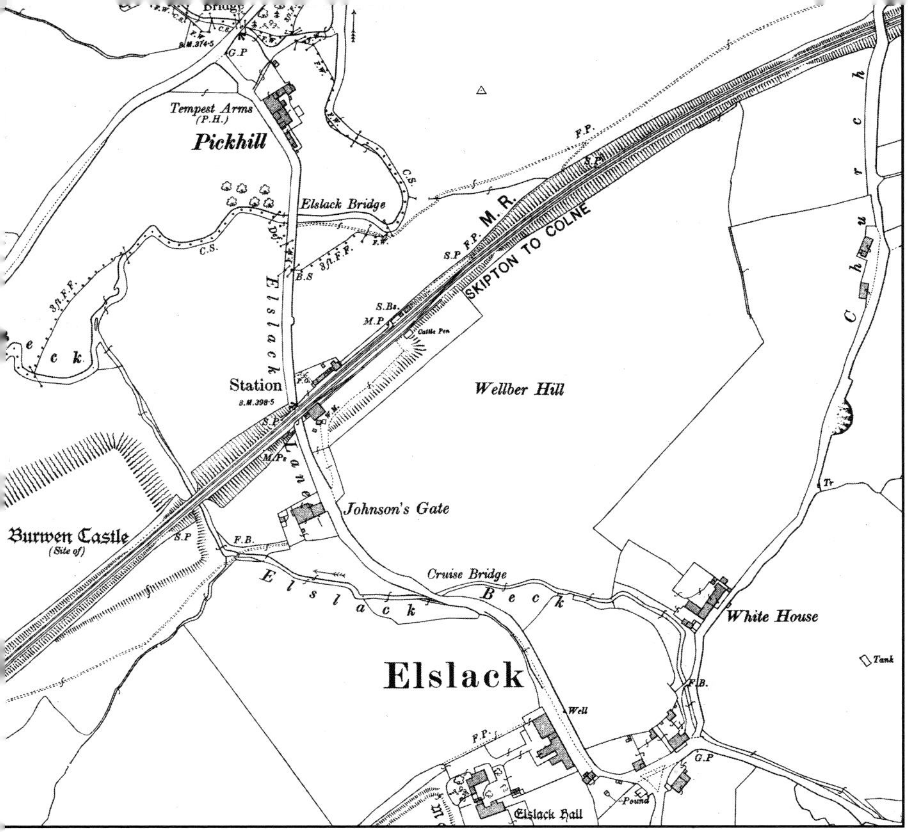

ELSLACK

XXXIX. Elslack village is historic, having a fort on a Roman road and being mentioned in the Domesday Book in 1086, but to this day it is a tiny settlement. However, when the Leeds and Bradford Extension Railway came through in 1848 a station was provided, just outside the main settlement. Staggered platforms were provided either side of the bridge over Elslack Lane, that for Colne trains being of lightweight timber construction, sited on the embankment. There was also a goods shed and single siding. Traffic was always light and the station an early casualty, closing to all traffic in 1952. It was perhaps unfortunate as Thornton-in-Craven, only 1½ miles away, was also little used but lasted until the line closed in 1970.

113. The original station building was moved to Elslack from Shipley, where it was inadequate for the traffic levels. This postcard from Midland Railway days shows the Skipton platform, with the main building and the station house beyond. The signal box and goods siding can also be seen but the goods shed is just off picture to the right. The lower quadrant signal is for westbound trains but sited on the outside of the curve, presumably to improve visibility for right-hand drive Midland Railway engines. There is an ironic bit of Yorkshire dialect on the postcard – 'Busy when tha gets there'. This was one station where that really was unlikely. After closure, but while the line remained open, the station remains lingered on but the site was cleared in the 1970s and is now occupied by business premises. (Lens of Sutton Association)

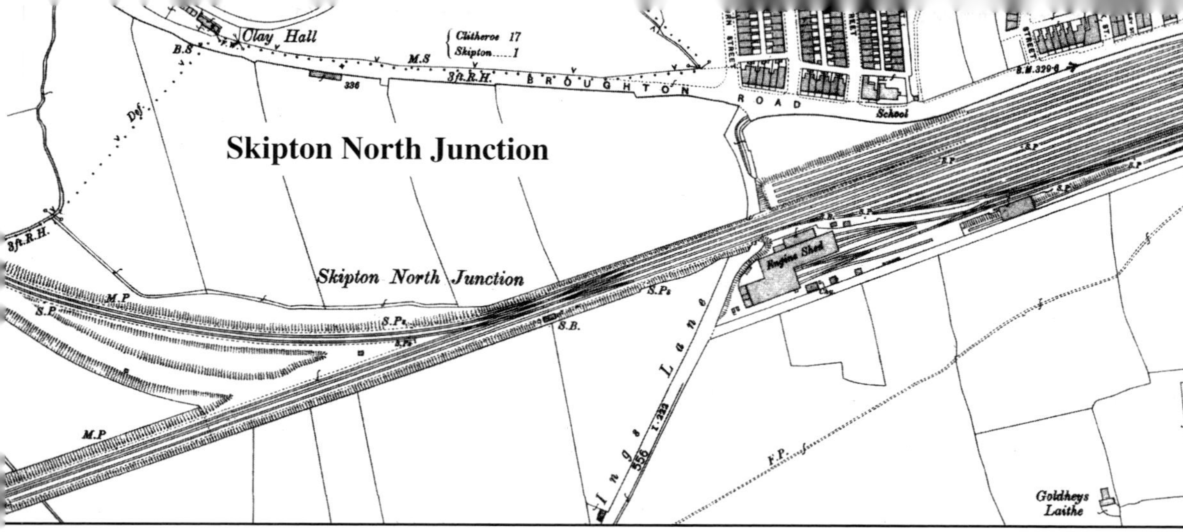

XL. At Skipton North Junction the line from Colne joined that from Settle Junction. The line from the north was originally the route of the 'Little' North Western Railway from Lancaster but later of course also the Settle and Carlisle Railway. As the two lines joined they continued to the station past the engine shed and numerous sidings. This map extract does not show the turntable at Skipton Shed, which was only installed when the depot was rebuilt in 1951 by BR.

114. Crab 2-6-0 no. 42888 runs along the up goods line at Skipton North Junction, arriving from the Settle Junction line on 27th September 1963. Its train appears to comprise all or mainly 16T mineral wagons. The lines in the foreground, heading left, are on the route to Colne and East Lancashire. No. 42888 was withdrawn from Lancaster Green Ayre shed in 1964 and so this train has probably worked to Skipton over the Little North Western route through Bentham. (Ernie's Railway Archives)

Skipton Shed

Skipton Shed, to the west of the station, opened in 1877 as a Midland Railway three road timber structure. It replaced an earlier L&BER shed near the station that operated since 1851. In 1892, a further three road timber building was added alongside the first, but slightly offset. The combined structure was rebuilt in brick by the LMR in 1951 and continued to service locomotives until closure on 3rd April 1967. After this the shed continued in use as a council depot, accessed from Engine Shed Lane. On starting to compile this album I planned to ask Craven Council for access to photograph any railway features, only to find that it had been demolished in 2021 and replaced by a modern office building – another missed opportunity.

115. LMS 'Jinty' 3F 0-6-0T no. 47454 on Skipton Shed in June 1964, in a view looking towards the station with the six road depot behind the camera. Now coded 10G in Carnforth District it had until 1963 been 24G in Accrington District. The turntable was installed during the 1951 rebuild of the depot. On another short siding stand two unidentified locomotives, a BR Standard 4MT 4-6-0 and a MR/LMS 4F 0-6-0. (F. Hornby courtesy ColourRail.co.uk)

116. There was probably a classic road coach parked on Engine Shed Lane on 29th July 1964 as these enthusiasts swarmed over Skipton Shed. This view looks back from the entrance roads towards the shed building and clearly shows the staggered nature of the building. Left to right we can see a WD 2-8-0, a 4F 0-6-0 and a 3F 0-6-0T grouped around the turntable and in the right hand shed a Stanier tender loco and a further 4F 0-6-0. Plenty of 'cops' for the spotters, next stop Hellifield or Rose Grove? (J.B. Hall courtesy ColourRail.co.uk)

117. Class 40 no. 40197 leaves Skipton up goods loop and approaches the station with the Heysham to Colwick petroleum tanks that routed via Wennington on 20th July 1976. The shed yard, tracks lifted, is on the left but the two-part shed is still standing. To the right the sidings are used for wagon repairs and examination, mainly stone trains from Rylstone Quarry near Grassington. Since 1976 the shed yard has accommodated commercial premises and the line from Leeds has been electrified, including the sidings on the right. These are now used for EMU stabling and light servicing, with wagon exams being undertaken at the quarry. (Tom Heavyside)

SKIPTON

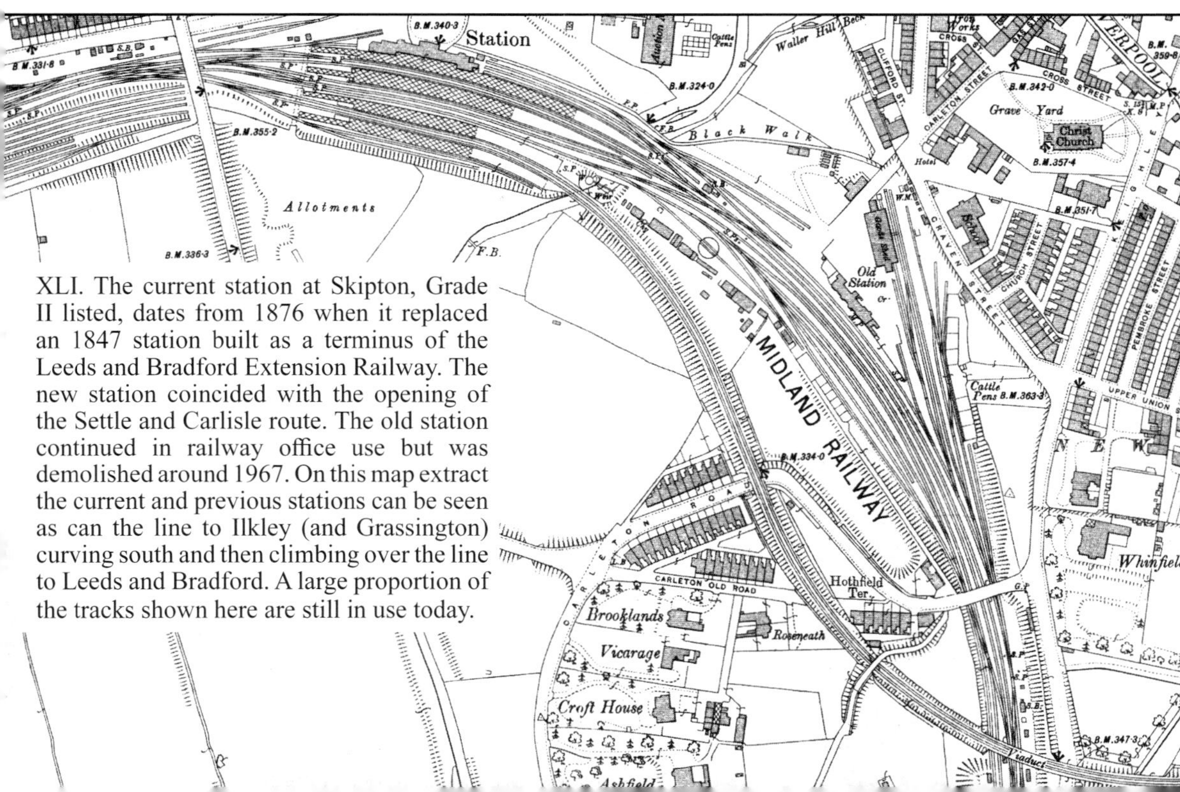

XLI. The current station at Skipton, Grade II listed, dates from 1876 when it replaced an 1847 station built as a terminus of the Leeds and Bradford Extension Railway. The new station coincided with the opening of the Settle and Carlisle route. The old station continued in railway office use but was demolished around 1967. On this map extract the current and previous stations can be seen as can the line to Ilkley (and Grassington) curving south and then climbing over the line to Leeds and Bradford. A large proportion of the tracks shown here are still in use today.

118. Black 5 no. 44673 leaves Skipton with a mixed rake of stock, heading north in May 1961. Six platforms were in use at this time, linked by subways, with the platforms on the far right, slightly elevated, serving the direct Ilkley line. In 1961 there were three possible main passenger routes for this train. An almost immediate turn west towards Colne, the Lancaster and Carnforth line (including the Ingleton and Low Gill branch) at Settle Junction, or the Settle and Carlisle line itself. No. 44673 was built at Horwich in February 1950, with experimental Skefco roller bearings on the driving axles. Withdrawn from Trafford Park at the end of May 1965, it was cut up at Crewe in August that year, reportedly the last steam locomotive scrapped at Crewe Works.
(D. Collins courtesy ColourRail.co.uk)

119. A Cravens class 113 hydraulic set at Skipton, probably around 1964. This will most likely have worked through from Manchester Victoria via Clifton Junction, Bury Bolton Street and Accrington. Although equipped with the four-character headcode panels these sets generally seemed to run with just two characters showing, like their more conventional (class 105) cousins. Whilst a view from this position today would show overhead wiring in place the station itself, and that magnificent canopy, are still there. The LMR maroon enamel signs have been replaced with modern equivalents, and the semaphore signal is no more but, 60 years on, this platform scene is otherwise little changed. (ColourRail.co.uk)

120. Since 2001, the Siemens class 333 EMUs have been used on the routes from Leeds to Skipton, Bradford and Ilkley. It is easy to forget that when these were first electrified in 1994-95 services were provided by class 308 trains that were over 30 years old and cascaded from the Great Eastern lines. This is unit no. 308157, in platform 2 at Skipton on 31st May 1997. They had been reduced from four cars to three for West Yorkshire but were getting very tired by this time. However, they lasted until 2001, with 308157 being one of the last in service. Even with electrification, Skipton has continued to see a variety of traction, with Pacer and Sprinter trains to Morecambe and Carlisle, freight services to and from the Settle and Carlisle line and Grassington branch and excursions, often steam hauled. Will that variety eventually include modern EMUs to Colne and beyond one day? (Martyn Hilbert)

Colne to Skipton reopening proposals: SELRAP

The line from Colne to Skipton should never have closed. It wasn't identified in the Beeching report and, even though the intermediate stations were not busy, it had potential as a through route between East Lancashire and West Yorkshire. However it was closed, in February 1970, and there have been various campaigns to reopen the route ever since.

Since 2001, the campaigning has been brought together, under the auspices of The Skipton to East Lancashire Rail Partnership (SELRAP).

Reinstatement will not be easy, with several key bridges needing rebuilding, and parts of the route blocked, but it will create a through route for passenger services, which could be electric trains running through from Leeds, calling at an intermediate station that would serve Earby and Barnoldswick. The reopened line would have a strategic role as it has also been proposed that freight trains, not least the Biomass services from the Port of Liverpool to Drax Power Station could be routed this way rather than their present hilly route through Cheshire and the Calder Valley.

SELRAP has over 500 members now, and has gathered support for the project from the local authorities and all the MPs covering the closed line and the still open routes on either side. The project to reopen is also supported by the East Lancashire Chamber of Commerce, Skipton Building Society, Peel Ports (Liverpool), Drax Power Station and other organisations.

The Partnership has had meetings with Ministers to press the case for reopening. It has highlighted the vast sums spent on rail projects in the south of England, already well-served, with the potential benefits that could be realised for far less by reopening the 12 miles from Colne to Skipton. Perhaps a future edition of this book will cover the reopening of this railway?

For more information, and to support the SELRAP campaign, visit *https://www.selrap.org.uk*

A
Abergavenny to Merthyr C 91 8
Abertillery & Ebbw Vale Lines D 84 5
Aberystwyth to Carmarthen E 90 1
Alnmouth to Berwick G 50 0
Alton - Branch Lines to A 11 6
Ambergate to Buxton G 28 9
Ambergate to Mansfield G 39 5
Andover to Southampton A 82 6
Ascot - Branch Lines around A 64 2
Ashburton - Branch Line to B 95 4
Ashford - Steam to Eurostar B 67 1
Ashford to Dover A 48 2
Austrian Narrow Gauge D 04 3
Avonmouth - BL around D 42 5
Aylesbury to Rugby D 91 3
B
Baker Street to Uxbridge D 90 6
Bala to Llandudno E 87 1
Banbury to Birmingham D 27 2
Banbury to Cheltenham E 63 5
Bangor to Holyhead F 01 7
Bangor to Portmadoc E 72 7
Barking to Southend C 80 2
Barmouth to Pwllheli E 53 6
Barry - Branch Lines around D 50 0
Bartlow - Branch Lines to F 27 7
Basingstoke to Salisbury A 89 4
Bath Green Park to Bristol C 36 9
Bath to Evercreech Junction A 60 4
Beamish 40 years on rails E94 9
Beattock to Carstairs G 84 5
Bedford to Wellingborough D 31 9
Berwick to Drem F 64 2
Berwick to St. Boswells F 75 8
B'ham to Tamworth & Nuneaton F 63 5
Birkenhead to West Kirby F 61 1
Birmingham to Wolverhampton E253
Blackburn to Hellifield F 95 6
Blackburn to Skipton G 85 2
Bletchley to Cambridge D 94 4
Bletchley to Rugby E 07 9
Bodmin - Branch Lines around B 83 1
Bolton to Preston G 61 6
Boston to Lincoln F 80 2
Bournemouth to Evercreech Jn A 46 8
Bradshaw's History F18 5
Bradshaw's Rail Times 1850 F 13 0
Branch Lines series - see town names
Brecon to Neath D 43 2
Brecon to Newport D 16 6
Brecon to Newtown E 06 2
Brighton to Eastbourne A 16 1
Brighton to Worthing A 03 1
Bristol to Taunton D 03 6
Bromley South to Rochester B 23 7
Bromsgrove to Birmingham D 87 6
Bromsgrove to Gloucester D 73 9
Broxbourne to Cambridge F16 1
Brunel - A railtour D 74 6
Bude - Branch Line to B 29 9
Burnham to Evercreech Jn B 68 0
Buxton to Stockport G 32 6
C
Cambridge to Ely D 55 5
Canterbury - BLs around B 58 9
Cardiff to Dowlais (Cae Harris) E 47 5
Cardiff to Pontypridd E 95 6
Cardiff to Swansea E 42 0
Carlisle to Beattock G 69 2
Carlisle to Hawick E 85 7
Carmarthen to Fishguard E 66 6
Caterham & Tattenham Corner B251
Central & Southern Spain NG E 91 8
Chard and Yeovil - BLs a C 30 7
Charing Cross to Orpington A 96 3
Cheddar - Branch Line to B 90 9
Cheltenham to Andover C 43 7
Cheltenham to Redditch D 81 4
Chesterfield to Lincoln G 21 0
Chester to Birkenhead F 21 5
Chester to Manchester F 51 2
Chester to Rhyl E 93 2
Chester to Warrington F 40 6
Chichester to Portsmouth A 14 7
Clacton and Walton - BLs to F 04 8
Clapham Jn to Beckenham Jn B 36 7
Cleobury Mortimer - BLs a E 18 5
Clevedon & Portishead - BLs to D180
Consett to South Shields E 57 4
Cornwall Narrow Gauge D 56 2
Corris and Vale of Rheidol E 65 9
Coventry to Leicester G 00 5
Craven Arms to Llandeilo E 35 2
Craven Arms to Wellington E 33 8
Crawley to Littlehampton A 34 5
Crewe to Manchester F 57 4
Crewe to Wigan G 12 8
Cromer - Branch Lines around C 26 0
Cromford and High Peak G 35 7
Croydon to East Grinstead B 48 0
Crystal Palace & Catford Loop B 87 1
Cyprus Narrow Gauge E 13 0
D
Darjeeling Revisited F 09 3
Darlington Leamside Newcastle E 28 4
Darlington to Newcastle D 98 2
Dartford to Sittingbourne B 34 3
Denbigh - Branch Lines around F 32 1
Derby to Chesterfield G 11 1
Derby to Nottingham G 45 6
Derby to Stoke-on-Trent F 93 2
Derwent Valley - BL to the D 06 7
Devon Narrow Gauge E 09 3
Didcot to Banbury D 02 9
Didcot to Swindon C 84 0
Didcot to Winchester C 13 0
Diss to Norwich G 22 7
Dorset & Somerset NG D 76 0
Douglas - Laxey - Ramsey E 75 8
Douglas to Peel C 88 8
Douglas to Port Erin C 55 0
Douglas to Ramsey D 39 5
Dover to Ramsgate A 78 9
Drem to Edinburgh G 06 7
Dublin Northwards in 1950s E 31 4
Dunstable - Branch Lines to E 27 7
E
Ealing to Slough C 42 0
Eastbourne to Hastings A 27 7
East Croydon to Three Bridges A 53 6
Eastern Spain Narrow Gauge E 56 7
East Grinstead - BLs to A 07 9
East Kent Light Railway A 61 1
East London - Branch Lines of C 44 4
East London Line B 80 0
East of Norwich - Branch Lines E 69 7
Effingham Junction - BLs a A 74 1
Ely to Norwich C 90 1
Enfield Town & Palace Gates D 32 6
Epsom to Horsham A 30 7
Eritrean Narrow Gauge E 38 3
Euston to Harrow & Wealdstone C 89 5
Exeter to Barnstaple B 15 2
Exeter to Newton Abbot C 49 9
Exeter to Tavistock B 69 5
Exmouth - Branch Lines to B 00 8
F
Fairford - Branch Line to A 52 9
Falmouth, Helston & St. Ives C 74 1
Fareham to Salisbury A 67 3
Faversham to Dover B 05 3
Felixstowe & Aldeburgh - BL to D 20 3
Fenchurch Street to Barking C 20 8
Festiniog - 50 yrs of enterprise C 83 3
Festiniog 1946-55 E 01 7
Festiniog in the Fifties B 68 8
Festiniog in the Sixties B 91 6
Ffestiniog in Colour 1955-82 F 25 3
Finsbury Park to Alexandra Pal C 02 8
French Metre Gauge Survivors F 88 8
Frome to Bristol B 77 0
G
Gainsborough to Sheffield G 17 3
Galashiels to Edinburgh F 52 9
Gloucester to Bristol D 35 7
Gloucester to Cardiff D 66 1
Gosport - Branch Lines around A 36 9
Greece Narrow Gauge D 72 2
Guildford to Redhill A 63 5
H
Hampshire Narrow Gauge D 36 4
Harrow to Watford D 14 2
Harwich & Hadleigh - BLs to F 02 4
Harz Revisited F 62 8
Hastings to Ashford A 37 6
Hawick to Galashiels F 36 9
Hawkhurst - Branch Line to A 66 6
Hayling - Branch Line to A 12 3
Hay-on-Wye - BL around D 92 0
Haywards Heath to Seaford A 28 4
Hemel Hempstead - BLs to D 88 3
Henley, Windsor & Marlow - BLa C77 2
Hereford to Newport D 54 8
Hertford & Hatfield - BLs a E 58 1
Hertford Loop E 71 0
Hexham to Carlisle D 75 3
Hexham to Hawick F 08 6
Hitchin to Peterborough D 07 4
Horsham - Branch Lines to A 02 4
Hull, Hornsea and Withernsea G 27 2
Hull to Scarborough G 60 9
Huntingdon - Branch Line to A 93 2
I
Ilford to Shenfield C 97 0
Ilfracombe - Branch Line to B 21 3
Ilkeston to Chesterfield G 26 5
Inverkeithing to Thornton Jct G 76 0
Ipswich to Diss F 81 9
Ipswich to Saxmundham C 41 3
Isle of Man Railway Journey F 94 9
Isle of Wight Lines - 50 yrs C 12 3
Italy Narrow Gauge F 17 8
K
Kent Narrow Gauge C 45 1
Kettering to Nottingham F 82-6
Kidderminster to Shrewsbury E 10 9
Kingsbridge - Branch Line to C 98 7
Kings Cross to Potters Bar E 62 8
King's Lynn to Hunstanton F 58 1
Kingston & Hounslow Loops A 83 3
Kingswear - Branch Line to C 17 8
L
Lambourn - Branch Line to C 70 3
Lancaster to Oxenholme G 77 7
Launceston & Princetown - BLs C 19 2
Leeds to Selby G 47 0
Leek - Branch Line From G 01 2
Leicester to Burton F 85 7
Leicester to Nottingham G 15 9
Lewisham to Dartford A 92 5
Lincoln to Cleethorpes F 56 7
Lincoln to Doncaster G 03 6
Lines around Newmarket G 54 8
Lines around Stamford F 98 7
Lines around Wimbledon B 75 6
Lines North of Stoke G 29 6
Liverpool to Runcorn G 72 2
Liverpool Street to Chingford D 01 2
Liverpool Street to Ilford C 34 5
Llandeilo to Swansea E 46 8
London Bridge to Addiscombe B 20 6
London Bridge to East Croydon A 58 1
Longmoor - Branch Lines to A 41 3
Looe - Branch Line to C 22 2
Loughborough to Ilkeston G 24 1
Loughborough to Nottingham F 68 0
Lowestoft - BLs around E 40 6
Ludlow to Hereford E 14 7
Lydney - Branch Lines around E 26 0
Lyme Regis - Branch Line to A 45 1
Lynton - Branch Line to B 04 6
M
Machynlleth to Barmouth E 54 3
Maesteg and Tondu Lines F 06 2
Majorca & Corsica Narrow Gauge F 41 3
Manchester to Bacup G 46 3
Manchester to Liverpool G 88 3
Mansfield to Doncaster G 23 4
March - Branch Lines around B 09 1
Market Drayton - BLs around F 67 3
Market Harborough to Newark F 86 4
Marylebone to Rickmansworth D 49 4
Melton Constable to Yarmouth Bch E031
Midhurst - Branch Lines of E 78 9
Midhurst - Branch Lines to F 00 0
Minehead - Branch Line to A 80 2
Monmouth - Branch Lines to E 20 8
Monmouthshire Eastern Valleys D 71 5
Moretonhampstead - BL to C 27 7
Moreton-in-Marsh to Worcester D 26 5
Morpeth to Bellingham F 87 1
Mountain Ash to Neath D 80 7
N
Newark to Doncaster F 78 9
Newbury to Westbury C 66 6
Newcastle to Alnmouth G 36 4
Newcastle to Hexham D 69 2
Newmarket to Haughley & Laxfield G 71 5
New Mills to Sheffield G 44 9
Newport (IOW) - Branch Lines to A 26 0
Newquay - Branch Lines to C 71 0
Newton Abbot to Plymouth C 60 4
Newtown to Aberystwyth E 41 3
Northampton to Peterborough F 92 5
North East German NG D 44 9
Northern Alpine Narrow Gauge F 37 6
Northern Spain Narrow Gauge E 83 3
North London Line B 94 7
North of Birmingham F 55 0
North of Grimsby - Branch Lines G 09 8
North Woolwich - BLs around C 65 9
Nottingham to Boston F 70 3
Nottingham to Kirkby Bentinck G 38 8
Nottingham to Lincoln F 43 7
Nottingham to Mansfield G 52 4
Nuneaton to Loughborough G 08 1
O
Ongar - Branch Line to E 05 5
Orpington to Tonbridge B 03 9
Oswestry - Branch Lines around E 60 4
Oswestry to Whitchurch E 81 9
Oxford to Bletchley D 57 9
Oxford to Moreton-in-Marsh D 15 9
P
Paddington to Ealing C 37 6
Paddington to Princes Risborough C819
Padstow - Branch Line to B 54 1
Peebles Loop G 19 7
Pembroke and Cardigan - BLs to F 29 1
Peterborough to Kings Lynn E 32 1
Peterborough to Lincoln F 89 5
Peterborough to Newark F 72 7
Plymouth - BLs around B 98 5
Plymouth to St. Austell C 63 5
Pontypool to Mountain Ash D 65 4
Pontypridd to Merthyr F 14 7
Pontypridd to Port Talbot E 86 4
Porthmadog 1954-94 - BLa B 31 2
Portmadoc 1923-46 - BLa B 13 8
Portsmouth to Southampton A 31 4
Portugal Narrow Gauge E 67 3
Potters Bar to Cambridge D 70 8
Preston & Lancaster - BLs around G 82 1
Preston to Blackpool G 16 6
Preston to the Fylde Coast G 81 4
Preston to Lancaster G 74 6
Princes Risborough - BL to D 05 0
Princes Risborough to Banbury C 85 7
R
Railways to Victory C 16 1
Reading to Basingstoke B 27 5
Reading to Didcot C 79 6
Reading to Guildford A 47 5
Redhill to Ashford A 73 4
Return to Blaenau 1970-82 C 64 2
Rhyl to Bangor F 15 4
Rhymney & New Tredegar Lines E 48 2
Rickmansworth to Aylesbury D 61 6
Romania & Bulgaria NG E 23 9
Ross-on-Wye - BLs around E 30 7
Ruabon to Barmouth E 84 0
Rugby to Birmingham E 37 6
Rugby to Loughborough F 12 3
Rugby to Stafford F 07 9
Rugeley to Stoke-on-Trent F 90 1
Ryde to Ventnor A 19 2
S
Salisbury to Westbury B 39 8
Salisbury to Yeovil B 06 0
Sardinia and Sicily Narrow Gauge F 50 5
Saxmundham to Yarmouth C 69 7
Saxony & Baltic Germany Revisited F 71 0
Saxony Narrow Gauge D 47 0
Scunthorpe to Doncaster G 34 0
Seaton & Sidmouth - BLs to A 95 6
Selsey - Branch Line to A 04 8
Sheerness - Branch Line to B 16 2
Sheffield towards Manchester G 18 0
Shenfield to Ipswich E 96 3
Shildon to Stockton G 79 1
Shrewsbury - Branch Line to A 86 4
Shrewsbury to Chester E 70 3
Shrewsbury to Crewe F 48 2
Shrewsbury to Ludlow E 21 5
Shrewsbury to Newtown E 29 1
Sirhowy Valley Line E 12 3
Sittingbourne to Ramsgate A 90 1
Skegness & Mablethorpe - BL to F 84 0
Slough to Newbury C 56 7
South African Two-foot gauge E 51 2
Southampton to Bournemouth A 42 0
Southend & Southminster BLs E 76 5
Southern Alpine Narrow Gauge F 22 2
South London Line B 46 6
South Lynn to Norwich City F 03 1
Southwold - Branch Line to A 15 4
Spalding - Branch Lines around E 52
Spalding to Grimsby F 65 9 6
Stafford to Chester F 34 5
Stafford to Wellington F 59 8
St Albans to Bedford D 08 1
St. Austell to Penzance C 67 3
St. Boswell to Berwick F 44 4
Stourbridge to Wolverhampton E 16
St. Pancras to Barking D 68 5
St. Pancras to Folkestone E 88 8
St. Pancras to St. Albans C 78 9
Stratford to Cheshunt F 53 6
Stratford-u-Avon to Birmingham D 77
Stratford-u-Avon to Cheltenham C 25
Sudbury - Branch Lines to F 19 2
Surrey Narrow Gauge C 87 1
Sussex Narrow Gauge C 68 0
Swaffham - Branch Lines around F 9
Swanage to 1999 - BL to A 33 8
Swanley to Ashford B 45 9
Swansea - Branch Lines around F 38
Swansea to Carmarthen E 59 8
Swindon to Bristol C 96 3
Swindon to Gloucester D 46 3
Swindon to Newport D 30 2
Swiss Narrow Gauge C 94 9
T
Talyllyn 60 E 98 7
Tamworth to Derby F 76 5
Taunton to Barnstaple B 60 2
Taunton to Exeter C 82 6
Taunton to Minehead F 39 0
Tavistock to Plymouth B 88 6
Tenterden - Branch Line to A 21 5
Three Bridges to Brighton A 35 2
Tilbury Loop C 86 4
Tiverton - BLs around C 62 8
Tivetshall to Beccles D 41 8
Tonbridge to Hastings A 44 4
Torrington - Branch Lines to B 37 4
Tourist Railways of France G 04 3
Towcester - BLs around E 39 0
Tunbridge Wells BLs A 32 1
U
Upwell - Branch Line to B 64 0
Uttoxeter to Macclesfield G 05 0
Uttoxeter to Buxton G 33 3
V
Victoria to Bromley South A 98 7
Victoria to East Croydon A 40 6
Vivarais Revisited E 08 6
W
Walsall Routes F 45 1
Wantage - Branch Line to D 25 8
Wareham to Swanage 50 yrs D 09 8
Watercress Line G 75 3
Waterloo to Windsor A 54 3
Waterloo to Woking A 38 3
Watford to Leighton Buzzard D 45 6
Wellingborough to Leicester F 73 4
Welshpool to Llanfair E 49 9
Wenford Bridge to Fowey C 09 3
Wennington to Morecambe G 58 6
Westbury to Bath B 55 8
Westbury to Taunton C 76 5
West Cornwall Mineral Rlys D 48 7
West Croydon to Epsom B 08 4
West German Narrow Gauge D 93 7
West London - BLs of C 50 5
West London Line B 84 8
West Somerset Railway G 78 4
West Wiltshire - BLs of D 12 8
Weymouth - BLs A 65 9
Willesden Jn to Richmond B 71 8
Wimbledon to Beckenham C 58 1
Wimbledon to Epsom B 62 6
Wimborne - BLs around A 97 0
Wirksworth - Branch Lines to G 10 4
Wisbech - BLs around C 01 7
Witham & Kelvedon - BLs a E 82 6
Woking to Alton A 59 8
Woking to Portsmouth A 25 3
Woking to Southampton A 55 0
Wolverhampton to Shrewsbury E 44
Wolverhampton to Stafford F 79 6
Worcester to Birmingham D 97 5
Worcester to Hereford D 38 8
Worthing to Chichester A 06 2
Wrexham to New Brighton F 47 5
Wroxham - BLs around F 31 4
Y
Yeovil - 50 yrs change C 38 3
Yeovil to Dorchester A 76 5
Yeovil to Exeter A 91 8
York to Scarborough F 23 9